A Preface to Paradise Lost

A Preface to Paradise Lost

Being the Ballard Matthews Lectures
Delivered at University College, North Wales, 1941

Revised and Enlarged

C.S. LEWIS, M.A.
Professor of Medieval and Renaissance English
Cambridge University

Introduction by
Mohit K. Ray

ATLANTIC
PUBLISHERS & DISTRIBUTORS (P) LTD

ATLANTIC
PUBLISHERS & DISTRIBUTORS (P) LTD
7/22, Ansari Road, Darya Ganj, New Delhi
Tel.: +91-11-4077 5252, 2327 3880
E-mail: orders@atlanticbooks.com
Web: www.atlanticbooks.com

Published by Atlantic Publishers & Distributors (P) Ltd., 2024
Reprint 2012, 2017, 2019, 2020, 2021, 2022, 2024

Printed & bound in India by Atlantic Print Services

Dedication

To Charles Williams

Dear Williams,

When I remember what kindness I received and what pleasure I had in delivering these lectures in the strange and beautiful hillside College at Bangor, I feel almost ungrateful to my Welsh hosts in offering this book not to them, but to you. Yet I cannot do otherwise. To think of my own lecture is to think of those other lectures at Oxford in which you partly anticipated, partly confirmed, and most of all clarified and matured, what I had long been thinking about Milton. The scene was, in a way, medieval, and may prove to have been historic. You were a *vagus* thrown among us by the chance of war. The appropriate beauties of the Divinity School provided your background. There we elders heard (among other things) what we had long despaired of hearing—a lecture on *Comus* which placed its importance where the poet placed it—and watched 'the yonge fresshe folkes, he or she,' who filled the benches listening first with incredulity, then with toleration, and finally with delight, to something so strange and new in their experience as the praise of chastity. Reviewers, who have not had time to re-read Milton, have failed for the most part to digest your criticism of him; but it is a reasonable hope that of those who heard you in Oxford many will understand henceforward that when the old poets made some virtue their theme they were not teaching but adoring, and that what we take for the didactic is often the enchanted. It gives me a sense of security to remember that, far from loving your work because you are my friend, I first sought your friendship because I loved your books. But for that, I should find it difficult to believe that your short *Preface*[1] to Milton is what it seems to

1. *The Poetical Works of Milton.* The World's Classics, 1940.

me to be—the recovery of a true critical tradition after more than a hundred years of laborious misunderstanding. The ease with which the thing was done would have seemed inconsistent with the weight that had to be lifted. As things are, I feel entitled to trust my own eyes. Apparently, the door of the prison was really unlocked all the time; but it was only you who thought of trying the handle. Now we can all come out.

Yours,

C.S. LEWIS

INTRODUCTION

A Preface to Paradise Lost was first delivered as Ballard Matthews Lectures at University College, North Wales in 1941. A revised and enlarged version of the lectures was published in book form by Oxford University Press in 1942.

It will be good to bear in mind some of the basic critical ideas of Lewis before we get down to his Preface. Lewis believes that literature is essentially a public activity through which the poet intends to move his readers by using a language the meanings and interpretations of which he shares with the readers. Lewis also would make a distinction between meaning and significance. Meaning inheres in what the text says or implies while significance is the way we relate the meaning to our other concerns. Accordingly for Lewis proper interpretation must be directed towards recognizing or identifying the original meaning, and criticism as a body of knowledge should 'enable a reader to enter more fully into the author's intentions.'

Lewis makes a distinction not between good and bad texts but between good and bad reading. The good reader receives the text while the bad reader only uses it. Good reading involves a sympathetic understanding which enables the reader to rise above self-interest and helps him/her to strengthen one of the most difficult of human capabilities. The argument is both Aristotelian and Christian in spirit. According to Aristotle an activity is 'good' when it brings out the highest qualities of the agent, and the moral virtue, analogous to good reading, is compassion or disinterested love which is Christian in spirit. Towards the end of *An Experiment of Criticism* Lewis writes: 'Good reading, therefore, though it is not essentially an affectional or moral or intellectual activity, has something in common with all three. In love, we escape from ourselves putting ourselves in other person's place and then transcending our own competitive particularity. In coming to understand anything we are rejecting the facts as they are for us in favour of the facts as they are[...]. Obviously this process can be described as an engagement or as a temporary annihilation of the self. But there is an old paradox: 'he that loseth his life shall save it.'

So, Lewis begins his Preface by reminding us that: '[the] first qualification for judging any piece of workmanship from a corkscrew to a cathedral is to know what it is—what it was *intended* to do and how it is meant to be used' (emphasis added). This is particularly important because 'the kind of poem Milton meant to write is unfamiliar to many readers.' So, in order to appreciate Milton it is necessary to put oneself in the place of Milton, as Lewis writes: 'The possible Lucretius in myself interests me more than the possible C.S. Lewis in Lucretius.' Lewis carefully makes a distinction between different kinds of epic—the classical and the romantic, and the Primary and the Secondary and holds that *solempne* or grandeur is a common aspect of all kinds of epic. Another obvious characteristic of an epic, because of its original oral form, is the repetition of common words, stock phrases, sometimes even whole lines, and Lewis contends that to 'a limited extent the technique of *Beowulf* is similar to Homer's.' The Secondary epic which 'aims at an even higher solemnity than the Primary' overcomes the difficulties arising out of the loss of the external aids to solemnity by an elevation of style and use of sonorous proper names.

In *Paradise Lost* the very first twenty-six lines give a sensation that 'some great thing is about to begin.' Milton uses a very complex syntax, no doubt; but the complexity of syntax is more than compensated by the simplicity of the imaginative effects that Milton is able to achieve.

Lewis believes that in his version of the Fall Milton follows St Augustine and argues that the Fall was due to Disobedience resulting from Pride. This is as much true of Satan as it is true of Eve. There is no point in arguing, as some critics have done, that Milton is a republican on earth but pleads for royalism in heaven, because as a believer in the Elizabethan view of the world order Milton holds that God has no 'natural superior.'

Lewis also very convincingly silences those critics who vociferously point out the differences between Milton's theological views expressed in *De Doctrina* and *Paradise Lost* when he insists that 'the sound course is to judge the poem *on its merits,* not to pre-judge it by reading doctrinal errors into the text,' and there is no doubt that in spite of the differences the poem remains 'overwhelmingly Christian.'

About Satan Lewis also subscribes to the general critical consensus that 'Satan is the best drawn of Milton's characters,' but he believes that it will, however, be a folly to fall victim to the charms of Satan and warns that to 'admire Satan is to give one's vote not only for a world of misery, but also for a world of lies and propaganda, of wishful thinking, of incessant autobiography.' About the followers of Satan Lewis holds that as in Homer every battle is described better than the previous one so about Satan's followers every character is drawn better than the previous character. About Milton's angels Lewis believes that instead of going into the great changes of philosophical thought from Scholasticism to the Platonic it is better to look upon the angels as 'poetizations of the glimpses which contemporary scientific imagination thought it had attained of a life going on just above the human level though normally inaccessible to direct observation.'

Lewis is not very happy about Milton's treatment of the sexuality of Adam and Eve and feels that Milton possibly was 'not aware of the magnitude of his own undertaking.'

Lewis, a fine critic and profound Milton scholar as he is, is not blind to the weaknesses of *Paradise Lost.* He believes, for example, that the poem suffers from structural flaws and that Milton's presentation of God is far from satisfactory, but in his balanced judgement he holds that in many respects it is better than the *Iliad* and the *Aeneid* as it 'records a real, irreversible, unrepeatable process in the history of the universe.' Lewis concludes with a fine dig at Eliot whose disparagement of Milton, at a particular stage of his critical career, was notorious: 'If Mr. Eliot disdains the eagles and trumpets of epic poetry because the fashion of this world passes away, I honour him. But if he goes on to draw the conclusion that all poetry should have the penitential qualities of his own best work, I believe he is mistaken.' It is really amazing how within a short span of just one hundred and thirty-one pages Lewis gives a lucid, insightful and succinct exposition to the *Paradise Lost,* calling critical attention to all the relevant and debatable aspects of the poem. Once armed with Lewis's Preface one can enter the formidable world of *Paradise Lost* without any fear or anxiety.

MOHIT K. RAY

Contents

Innumerabilli immortali
Disegualmente in lor letizia eguali:
Tasso, *Gier, Lib,* ix, 57

How so many learned heads should so far forget their metaphysicks, and destroy the ladder and scale creatures.

Browne, Rel. Med. I, XXX.

1

Epic Poetry

> A perfect judge will read each work of wit
> With the same spirit that its author writ.
>
> —POPE.

The first qualification for judging any piece of workmanship from a corkscrew to a cathedral is to know *what* it is—what it was intended to do and how it is meant to be used. After that has been discovered the temperance reformer may decide that the corkscrew was made for a bad purpose, and the communist may think the same about the cathedral. But such questions come later. The first thing is to understand the object before you: as long as you think the corkscrew was meant for opening tins or the cathedral for entertaining tourists you can say nothing to the purpose about them. The first thing the reader needs to know about *Paradise Lost* is what Milton meant it to be.

This need is specially urgent in the present age because the kind of poem Milton meant to write is unfamiliar to many readers. He is writing epic poetry which is a species of narrative poetry, and neither the species nor the genus is very well understood at present. The misunderstanding of the genus (narrative poetry) I have learned from looking into used copies of our great narrative poems. In them you find often enough a number of not very remarkable lines underscored with pencil in the first two pages, and all the rest of the book virgin. It is easy to see what has happened. The unfortunate reader has set out expecting 'good lines'—little ebullient patches of delight—such as he is accustomed to find in lyrics, and has thought he was finding them in things that took his fancy for accidental reasons during the first five minutes; after that, finding that the poem cannot really be read in this way, he has given it up. Of the continuity of a long narrative poem, the subordination of the line to the paragraph and the paragraph to the Book and even of the Book to the whole, of the grand sweeping effects that take a quarter of an hour to develop themselves, he has had no conception. The misunderstanding of the species (epic narrative) I have learned from the errors of critics, including myself, who sometimes regard as faults in *Paradise Lost* those very properties which the poet laboured hardest to attain and which, rightly enjoyed, are essential to its specific delightfulness (οἰκεία ἡδονή). Our study of Milton's epic must therefore begin with a study of epic in general.

I anticipate two incidental advantages from this procedure. In the first place, as we shall see, this approach was Milton's own. The first question he asked himself was not 'What do I want to say ?' but 'What *kind* of poem do I want to make ?'—to which of the great pre-existing *kinds*, so different in the expectations they excite and fulfil, so diverse in their powers, so recognizably distinguished in the minds of all cultured readers, do I intend to contribute ? The parallel is not to be found in a modern author considering what his unique message is and what unique idiom will best convey it, but rather in a gardener asking whether he will make a rockery *or* a tennis court, an architect asking whether he is to make a church *or* a house, a boy debating whether to play hockey *or* football, a man hesitating between marriage and celibacy. The things between which choice is to be made already exist in their own right, each with a character of its own well established in the public world and governed by its own laws. If you choose one, you lose the specific beauties and delights of the other: for your aim is not mere excellence, but the excellence proper to the thing chosen—the goodness of a rockery or a celibate being different from that of a tennis court or a husband. In the second place, this approach will force us to attend to that aspect of poetry which is now most neglected. Every poem can be considered in two ways—as what the poet has to say, and as a *thing* which he *makes*. From the one point of view it is an expression of opinions and emotions; from the other, it is an organization of words which exist to produce a particular kind of patterned experience in the readers. Another way of stating this duality would be to say that every poem has two parents—its mother being the mass of experience, thought, and the like, inside the poet, and its father the pre-existing Form (epic, tragedy, the novel, or what not) which he meets in the public world. By studying only the mother, criticism becomes one-sided. It is easy to forget that the man who writes a good love sonnet needs not only to be enamoured of a woman, but also to be enamoured of the Sonnet. It would, in my opinion, be the greatest error to suppose that this fertilization of the poet's internal matter by the pre-existing Form impairs his originality, in any sense in which originality is a high literary excellence. (It is the smaller poets who invent forms, insofar as forms are invented.) *Materia appetit formam ut virum femina*. The matter inside the poet *wants* the Form: in submitting to the Form it becomes really original, really the origin of great work. The attempt to be oneself often brings out only the more conscious and superficial parts of a man's mind; working to produce a given kind of poem which will present a given theme as justly, delightfully, and lucidly as possible, he is more likely to bring out all that was really in him, and much of which he himself had no suspicion. That concentration on the male parent of *Paradise Lost*, the Epic Form, which I intend to practise is the more desirable because excellent helps to the study of the raw material inside the poet—the experiences, character, and opinions of the man Milton—already exist in the work of Miss Darbishire and Dr. Tillyard.

Milton's own approach is to be learned from a passage in the Preface to the *Reason of Church Government*, Book II (Bohn's Edn., Vol. II, 478). The question before him is whether to write (A) an Epic; (B) a Tragedy; (C) a Lyric. The discussion of (A) begins with the words 'whether that epic form:' the discussion of (B) with 'or whether those dramatic constitutions;' that of (C) with 'or if occasion shall lead.' The whole scheme may be set out as follows:

(A) Epic.
- I. (a) The diffuse Epic [Homer, Virgil, and Tasso].
  - (b) The brief Epic [the Book of Job].
- II. (a) Epic keeping the rules of Aristotle.
  - (b) Epic following Nature.
- III. Choice of subject ['what king or knight before the conquest'].

(B) Tragedy.
- (a) On the model of Sophocles and Euripides.
- (b) On the model of *Canticles* or the *Apocalypse.*

(C) Lyric.
- (a) On the Greek model ['Pindarus and Callimachus'].
- (b) On Hebrew models ['Those frequent songs throughout the Law and the Prophets'].

(A), the Epic, is our primary concern, but before we consider it in detail one feature which runs through the whole scheme demands our attention. It will be noticed that Classical and Scriptural models are mentioned under each of the three heads, and under one head, that of tragedy, the Biblical model seems to be dragged in, as they say, 'by the heels.' This is less true of the Biblical model for epic. Milton's classification of *Job* as a sub-species of epic (with the *differentia* 'brief') may be novel, but it is reasonable, and I have no doubt at all that this is the form he believed himself to be practising in *Paradise Regained*, which has affinities to *Job* in its theme as well as in its lay-out. Under the third heading (Lyric) the Hebrew models come in with perfect propriety, and here Milton has added an interesting note. Almost as if he had foreseen an age in which 'Puritanism' should be the bear seen in every bush, he has given his opinion that Hebrew lyrics are better than Greek 'not in their divine argument alone, but in the very critical art of composition.' That is, he has told us that his preference for the Hebrew is not only moral and religious, but aesthetic also.[1] I once had a pupil,

1. The unpopular passage in *P.R.* iv, 347 ('*Sion's* songs to all true tasts excelling') is better understood if we remember that it reflects a literary opinion which Milton had, in some form or other, held all his life.

innocent alike of the Greek and of the Hebrew tongue, who did not think himself thereby disqualified from pronouncing this judgement a proof of Milton's bad taste; the rest of us, whose Greek is amateurish and who have no Hebrew, must leave Milton to discuss the question with his peers. But if any man will read aloud on alternate mornings for a single month a page of Pindar and a page of the Psalms in any translation he chooses, I think I can guess which he will first grow tired of.

Warned by what Milton has said under the heading of Lyric, I would not hastily conclude that the Biblical models throughout the scheme represent the victory of his 'Puritanism' over his 'Classicism.' Indeed it would be almost equally plausible to put the matter the other way round. If a strict Classicist might resent the intrusion of the Biblical models, a strict 'Puritan' might equally resent the degradation of the Word of God to the status of a source of precedents for literary composition—as if it were *on a level* with the work of uninspired and even heathen poets. The truth probably is that there is no struggle, and therefore no victory on either side. There is *fusion,* or integration. The Christian and the classical elements are not being kept in watertight compartments, but being organized together to produce a whole.

Let us now consider Milton's (A), the Epic. His distinction between 'Diffuse' and 'Brief' has already been referred to. More difficult is his contrast between following Aristotle and following Nature. The 'rules' of Aristotle for Epic, insofar as they are relevant here, amount to the precept of *unity.* The epic poet must deal with a single action, like Homer (*Poetics,* cap. 23): those who thought that all the adventures of Theseus would make one poem because Theseus was one man were mistaken. In Milton's mind there is apparently some other kind of epic contrasted with that which Aristotle recommended, and this other kind is oddly regarded as following 'nature'; oddly, because later classicists tended to identify nature with the 'rules.' Now there was only one thing known to Milton which bore the name of epic and also differed in kind from the work of Homer and Virgil—the romantic or chivalrous epic of Boiardo, Ariosto, and Spenser. This differs from the ancient works, firstly by its lavish use of the marvellous, secondly by the place given to love, and thirdly by the multiple action of interwoven stories. The third characteristic is the most immediately noticeable of the three, and I believe that it is what Milton is mainly referring to. It is not at first apparent why he should call it a following of nature. I am pretty sure that the complete answer to the question is to be found somewhere in the Italian critics; but in the meantime something like an answer I have found in Tasso. In his *Discourses on the Heroic Poem* Tasso raises the whole problem of multiplicity or unity in an epic plot, and says that the claims of unity are supported by Aristotle, the ancients, and Reason, but those of multiplicity by usage, the actual taste of all knights and ladies, and Experience (*op. cit.,* III). By 'experience' he doubtless means such unhappy experiences as that of his father who wrote an *Amadis* in strict conformity to the rules of Aristotle, but found that the recitation of it emptied the auditorium, from which 'he concluded that unity of action was a thing affording little pleasure.' Now usage and experience, especially when contrasted with precedent and reason, are concepts not very far from 'Nature.' I believe, therefore, with very little doubt, that Milton's hesitation between 'the rules of Aristotle' and 'following Nature' means, in simpler language, 'shall I write an epic in twelve books with a simple plot, or shall I write something in stanzas and cantos about knights and ladies and enchantments?' The importance of this explanation, if true, is threefold.

1. Connecting it with his ideas of a possible theme ('what king or knight before the conquest'), we may surmise that the romantic subject was rejected at about the same time as the romantic *form,* the Spenserian or Italian type of epic. We tend perhaps to assume that if Milton's *Arthuriad* had been written it would have been the same *sort* of poem as *Paradise Lost,* but surely this is very rash? A much more Spenserian Milton—the Milton of *L'Allegro, Il Penseroso,* and *Comus*—had to be partially repressed before *Paradise Lost* could be written: if you choose the rockery you must abandon the tennis court. It is very likely that if Arthur had been chosen the Spenserian Milton would have grown to full development and the actual Milton, the 'Miltonic' Milton, would have been repressed.

There is evidence that Milton's ideas for an *Arthuriad* were very 'romantic' indeed. He was going to paint Arthur *etiam sub terris bella moventem (Mansus,* 81), Arthur's wars 'beneath the earth.' I do not know whether this means strange adventures experienced by Arthur in some other world between his disappearance in the barge and his predicted return to help the Britons at their need, or adventures in fairyland before he became king, or some even wilder Welsh tale about the caldron of Hades. But it certainly does not suggest the purely heroic and military epic which we are apt to think of when Milton's Arthurian projects are mentioned.

2. Milton's hesitation between the classical and the romantic types of epic is one more instance of something which runs through all his work; I mean the co-existence, in a live and sensitive tension, of apparent opposites. We have already noted the fusion of Pagan and Biblical interests in his very map of poetry. We shall have occasion, in a later section, to notice, side by side with his rebelliousness, his individualism, and his love of liberty, his equal love of discipline, of hierarchy, of what Shakespeare calls 'degree.' From the account of his early reading in *Smectymnuus* we gather a third tension. His first literary loves, both for their style and their matter, were the erotic (indeed the almost pornographic) elegiac poets of Rome: from them he graduated to the idealized love poetry of Dante and Petrarch and of 'those lofty fables which recount in solemn cantos the deeds of knighthood': from these to the philosophical sublimation of sexual passion in 'Plato and his equal (*i.e.* his contemporary) Xenophon.' An original voluptuousness greater, perhaps, than that of any English poet, is pruned, formed, organized, and made human by progressive purifications, themselves the responses to a quite equally intense aspiration—an equally imaginative and emotional aspiration—towards chastity. The modern idea of a Great Man is one who stands at the lonely extremity of some single line of development—one either as pacific as Tolstoy or as military as Napoleon, either as clotted as Wagner or as angelic as Mozart. Milton is certainly not that kind of great man. He is a great *Man*. '*On ne montre pas sa grandeur,*' says Pascal, '*pour être à une extrémité, mais bien en touchant les deux à la fois et remplissant tout l'entre-deux.*'

3. By observing how Milton subdivides the Epic into its sub-species, we are again brought face to face with the problem of Forms—with the virginal *materia* inside the poet hesitating, as it were, between different suitors. When he wrote the *Reason of Church Government* the different types of poem were all present to Milton's mind, all different, all attractive, each offering its own unique opportunities, but each also demanding peculiar sacrifices. His sentence about epic is really a short history of epic poetry. To know what he was talking about, to feel as he felt, and so, in the end, to know what he was really choosing when he finally chose and what kind of thing he was making when he acted on that final choice, we also must attend to epic. The biography of the literary kind will help our reading of *Paradise Lost* at least as much as the biography of the poet.

2
Is Criticism Possible?

> *Amicus Plato*, my father would say, construing the words to my uncle Toby as he went along, *Amicus Plato*; that is, Dinah was my aunt—*sed magis amica veritas*—but truth is my sister.
>
> —*Tristram Shandy*, Vol. 1, cap. 21.

But, first, a necessary digression. A recent remark of Mr. Eliot's poses for us at the outset the fundamental question whether we (mere critics) have any right to talk about Milton at all. Mr. Eliot says bluntly and frankly that the best contemporary practising poets are the only 'jury of judgement'[1] whose verdict on his own views of *Paradise Lost* he will accept. And Mr. Eliot is here simply rendering explicit a notion that has become increasingly prevalent for about a hundred years—the notion that poets are the only judges of poetry. If I make Mr. Eliot's words the peg on which to hang a discussion of this notion it must not, therefore, be assumed that this is, for me, more than a convenience, still less that I wish to attack him *quâ* Mr. Eliot. Why should I? I agree with him about matters of such moment that all literary questions are, in comparison, trivial.

Let us consider what would follow if we took Mr. Eliot's view seriously. The first result is that I, not being one of the best contemporary poets, cannot judge Mr. Eliot's criticism at all. What then shall I do? Shall I go to the best contemporary poets, who can, and ask them whether Mr. Eliot is right? But in order to go to them I must first know who they are. And this, by hypothesis, I cannot find out; the same lack of poethood

1. *A Note on the Verse of John Milton. Essays and Studies*, Vol. XXI, 1936.

which renders my critical opinions on Milton worthless renders my opinions on Mr. Pound or Mr. Auden equally worthless. Shall I then go to Mr. Eliot and ask him to tell me who the best contemporary poets are ? But this, again, will be useless. I personally may think Mr. Eliot a poet—in fact, I do—but then, as he has explained to me, my thoughts on such a point are worthless. I cannot find out whether Mr. Eliot is a poet or not; and until I have found out I cannot know whether his testimony to the poethood of Mr. Pound and Mr. Auden is valid. And for the same reason I cannot find out whether *their* testimony to *his* poethood is valid. Poets become on this view an unrecognizable society (an Invisible Church), and their mutual criticism goes on within a closed circle which no outsider can possibly break into at any point.

But even within the circle it is no better. Mr. Eliot is ready to accept the verdict of the best contemporary poets on his criticism. But how does *he* recognize them as poets? Clearly, because he is a poet himself; for if he is not, his opinion is worthless. At the basis of his whole critical edifice, then, lies the judgement 'I am a poet.' But this is a critical judgement. It therefore follows that when Mr. Eliot asks himself, 'Am I a poet?' he has to *assume* the answer 'I am' before he can *find* the answer 'I am;' for the answer, being a piece of criticism, is valuable only *if* he is a poet. He is thus compelled to beg the question before he can get started at all. Similarly Mr. Auden and Mr. Pound must beg the question before *they* get started. But since no man of high intellectual honour can base his thought on an exposed *petitio* the real result is that no such man can criticize poetry at all, neither his own poetry nor that of his neighbour. The republic of letters resolves itself into an aggregate of uncommunicating and unwindowed monads; each has unawares crowned and mitred himself Pope and King of Pointland.

In answer to this Mr. Eliot may properly plead that the same apparently vicious circle meets us in other maxims which I should find it less easy to reject: as when we say that only a good man can judge goodness, or only a rational man can judge reasonings, or only a doctor can judge medical skill. But we must beware of false parallels. (1) In the *moral* sphere, though insight and performance are not strictly equal (which would make both guilt and aspiration impossible), yet it is true that continued disobedience to conscience makes conscience blind. But disobedience to conscience is voluntary; bad poetry, on the other hand, is usually not made on purpose. The writer was trying to make good poetry. He was endeavouring to follow such lights as he had—a procedure which in the moral sphere is the pledge of progress, but not in poetry. Again, a man may fall outside the class of 'good poets' not by being a bad poet, but by writing no poetry at all, whereas at every moment of his waking life he is either obeying or breaking the moral law. The moral blindness consequent on being a bad man must therefore fall on every one who is not a good man, whereas the critical blindness (if any) due to being a bad poet need by no means fall on every one who is not a good poet. (2) *Reasoning* is never, like poetry, judged *from the outside* at all. The critique of a chain of reasoning is itself a chain of reasoning: the critique of a tragedy is not itself a tragedy. To say that only the rational man can judge reasonings is, therefore, to make the merely analytical proposition 'Only the rational man can reason,' parallel to 'only the poet can make poetry,' or 'only the critic can criticize,' and not at all parallel to the synthetic proposition 'only the poet can criticize.' (3) As regards a *skill*, such as medicine or engineering, we must distinguish. Only the skilled can judge the skilfulness, but that is not the same as judging the value of the result. It is for cooks to say whether a given dish proves skill in the cook; but whether the product on which this skill has been lavished is worth eating or no is a question on which a cook's opinion is of no particular value. We may therefore allow poets to tell us (at least if they are experienced in the same *kind* of composition) whether it is easy or difficult to write like Milton, but not whether the reading of Milton is a valuable experience. For who can endure a doctrine which would allow only dentists to say whether our teeth were aching, only cobblers to say whether our shoes hurt us, and only governments to tell us whether we were being well governed?

Such are the results if we take the position in its full rigour. But of course if it is only meant that a good poet, other things being equal (which they often are not), is reasonably likely, in talking about the kinds of poetry he has himself written well and read with delight, to say something more worth hearing than another, then we need not deny it.

3

Primary Epic

Then the first cors come with crakkyng of trumpes,
With mony baner ful bryght that therbi henged;
Newe nakryn noyse with the noble pipes,
Wylde werbles and wyght wakned lote,
That mony hert ful highe hef at her towches.
—*Sir Gawayn and the Grene Knyght,* 116.

The older critics divided Epic into Primitive and Artificial, which is unsatisfactory, because no surviving ancient poetry is really primitive and all poetry is in some sense artificial. I prefer to divide it into Primary Epic and Secondary Epic—the adjectives being purely chronological and implying no judgements of value. The *secondary* here means not 'the second rate,' but what comes after, and grows out of, the *primary*.

The Primary Epic will be illustrated from the Homeric poems and from the English *Beowulf,* and our effort here, as throughout the present discussion, will be to discover what sort of thing the Primary Epics were, how they were meant to be used, what expectations they hoped to satisfy. But at the very outset a distinction must be made. Both *Beowulf* and the Homeric poems, besides being poetry themselves, describe poetical performances, at feasts and the like, proceeding in the world which they show us. From these descriptions we can gather what the epic was in a heroic age; but it does not follow that *Beowulf* and the Homeric poems are themselves the same kind of thing. They may or may not *be* what they *describe.* We must therefore distinguish the literary conditions attributed to the heroic age within the surviving poems, which, since they are described, can be studied, from the literary conditions in which the surviving poems were themselves produced, which can only be conjectured. I proceed, then, to some account of the literary conditions which Homer *describes*.

All poetry is oral, delivered by the voice, not read, and, so far as we are told, not written either. And all poetry is musical. The poet delivers it to the accompaniment of some instrument (*phorminx* and *kithara* are the names given to it—or them). But I think we detect within this oral poetry two kinds—a popular poetry, and a court poetry. We read in one place how 'merry boys and girls (at a vintage) carried the sweet fruit in baskets, and amidst them a youth played on the stringed instrument that moves desire and sang the sweet song called *Linos*' (Il. XVIII, 569). Or again, we read of a dancing floor where 'boys and girls danced hand in hand and amidst them sang the minstrel while two tumblers whirled in the centre' (Il. *ibid.*, 593 et seq.). There is no suggestion of the court in either passage. If we now turn to scenes at court we find two things going on, of which the first may or may not be different from the popular poetry, but which are certainly quite different from each other. In the first, the court poet gets up, steps into a central position in the midst of a troupe of expert dancers and sings a short lay which has the three characteristics of being about gods not men, of being comic, and of being indecent. That is the light court poetry (*Od.* VIII, 256-65). The serious court poetry is another matter. The poet has a chair placed for him and an instrument put into his hands. A table is set beside him with wine, that he may drink 'when his heart desires.' Presently, without orders from the king, he begins his lay when the Muse prompts him; its three characteristics are that it is about men, it is historically true, and it is tragic (*Od.* VIII, 62-75).

The important point to notice is that of the three kinds of performance mentioned only the last is epic. Primary Epic is not to be identified with 'oral poetry of the heroic age,' or even with 'oral court poetry.' It is *one* of the different kinds of poetry heard in a heroic court. Its sharp distinction from lighter kinds makes less impression on us than it should because we merely read about it. If we had *seen* the poet, first ordered to get up and take his place in a comic and indecent ballet, and then, seated and honoured with wine and spontaneously beginning his tragic lay at the inner prompting of a goddess, we should never again forget the distinction.

Turning to *Beowulf*, we find a slightly different situation. We hear nothing at all in this poem about poetry outside the court. But we can supplement *Beowulf* from other sources. In Bede's account of Caedmon (*Eccl. His.* IV, 24) we get the glimpse of a feast among men apparently of peasant's rank, where each sang in turn as the harp came to him. It is just conceivable that what each sang was a very short heroic lay, but there is no reason to suppose this. Certainly the Anglo-Saxons had songs of a very different type. Alcuin's letter to Hygebald in 797 is always quoted because, in deploring the use of heathen poetry in religious houses, he mentions *Hinieldus* who is probably Hrothgar's son-in-law Ingeld. But it should also be remembered that he asks for 'the voice of the reader in the house rather than the laughter of the mob in the streets' (*voces legentium in domibus tuis non ridentium turvam in plateis*). This 'laughter' would not be connected with heroic lays. No doubt, Alcuin may be referring to ribald conversation and not to poetry at all. But it seems to me very likely that he means comic poetry, and that comic, or at least light, poems were sung at the feast which Caedmon attended. This is admittedly conjecture; but it would be very odd if the ancestors of Chaucer, Shakespeare, Dickens, and Mr. Jacobs produced no funny stories.

When we turn to *Beowulf's* picture of the court we are on surer ground. In lines 2105 and following we have a performance given by Hrothgar himself. We learn that he sometimes (*hwilum*) produced a *gidd* or lay which was *sop* and *sarlic* (true and tragic), sometimes a tale of wonders (*sellic spell*), and sometimes, with the fetters of age heavy upon him, he began to recall his youth, the strength that once was his in battle; his heart swelled within him as he remembered the vanished winters. Professor Tolkien has suggested to me that this is an account of the complete range of court poetry, in which three kinds of poem can be distinguished—the lament for mutability (*hu seo prag gewat*) now represented by the *Wanderer* and the *Seafarer*, the tale of strange adventures, and the 'true and tragic' lay such as the *Finnsburg* poem, which alone is true epic. *Beowulf* itself contains

elements of the *sellic spell,* but it is certainly *sarlic* and probably much of it was regarded as *sop.* Without pressing these distinctions too far, we can certainly conclude from this passage that the author of *Beowulf* is aware of different kinds of court poetry. Here, as in Homer, Epic does not mean simply whatever was sung in hall. It is one of the possible entertainments, marked off from the others, in Homer by the spontaneity and quasi-oracular character of the poet's performance, and in both Homer and *Beowulf* by tragic quality, by supposed historical truth, and by the gravity that goes with 'true tragedy.'

Such, then, is epic as we first hear of it; the loftiest and gravest among the kinds of court poetry in the oral period, a poetry *about* nobles, made *for* nobles, and performed on occasion, *by* nobles (cf. *Il.* IX, 189). We shall go endlessly astray if we do not get well fixed in our minds at the outset the picture of a venerable figure, a king, a great warrior, or a poet inspired by the Muse, seated and chanting to the harp a poem on high matters before an assembly of nobles in a court, at a time when the court was the common centre of many interests which have since been separated; when it was not only the Windsor Castle, but also the Somerset House, the Horseguards, the Covent Garden, and perhaps even, in certain respects, the Westminster Abbey, of the tribe. But also, it was the place of festivity, the place of brightest hearths and strongest drink, of courtesy, merriment, news, and friendship. All this is a long way from Mr. John Milton printing a book to be sold in seventeenth-century London, but it is not irrelevant. From its early association with the heroic court there comes into Epic Poetry a quality which survives, with strange transformations and enrichments, down to Milton's own time, and it is a quality which moderns find difficult to understand. It has been split up, or dissociated, by recent developments, so that we now have to represent it by piecing together what seem to us quite unconnected ideas, but are really fragments of that old unity.

This quality will be understood by any one who really understands the meaning of the Middle English word *solempne.* This means something different, but not quite different, from modern English *solemn.* Like *solemn* it implies the opposite of what is familiar, free and easy, or ordinary. But unlike *solemn* it does not suggest gloom, oppression, or austerity. The ball in the first act of *Romeo and Juliet* was a 'solemnity.' The feast at the beginning of *Gawain and the Green Knight* is very much of a solemnity. A great mass by Mozart or Beethoven is as much a solemnity in its hilarious *gloria* as in its poignant *crucifixus est*. Feasts are, in this sense, *more* solemn than fasts. Easter is *solempne*, Good Friday is not. The *Solempne* is the festal which is also the stately and the ceremonial, the proper occasion for *pomp*—and the very fact that *pompous* is now used only in a bad sense measures the degree to which we have lost the old idea of 'solemnity.' To recover it you must think of a court ball, or a coronation, or a victory march, as these things appear to people who *enjoy* them; in an age when every one puts on his oldest clothes to be happy in, you must re-awake the simpler state of mind in which people put on gold and scarlet to be happy in. Above all, you must be rid of the hideous idea, fruit of a widespread inferiority complex, that pomp, on the proper occasions, has any connexion with vanity or self-conceit. A celebrant approaching the altar, a princess led out by a king to dance a minuet, a general officer on a ceremonial parade, a major-domo preceding the boar's head at a Christmas feast—all these wear unusual clothes and move with calculated dignity. This does not mean that they are vain, but that they are obedient; they are obeying the *hoc age* which presides over every solemnity. The modern habit of doing ceremonial things unceremoniously is no proof of humility; rather it proves the offender's inability to forget himself in the rite, and his readiness to spoil for every one else the proper pleasure of ritual.

This is the first fence we must get over. Epic, from the beginning, is *solempne*. You are to expect pomp. You are to 'assist,' as the French say, at a great festal action. I have stressed the point at this early stage because misunderstandings must be eradicated from the very first. But our history of Epic has so far brought us only to the germ of epic *solemnity*. The Epic does not decline from the lay in the heroic court to the Miltonic level, but rises; it accumulates and enriches *solemnity* as the centuries proceed.

So much for the poems mentioned in Homer and *Beowulf*,

but what of Homer and *Beowulf* themselves? Are they also oral court poetry of the kind described?

Whether 'Homer' is oral poetry or not is a question that can be answered with great probability. It must not, of course, be confused by identifying 'oral' or recited poetry with anonymous poetry, still less with folk poetry. Mr. Nilsson tells us of a modern poet in Sumatra who spent five years on the composition of a single poem, though he could neither read nor write (*Homer and Mycenae,* cap. V). The question whether the *Iliad* is oral poetry is quite separate from the question of authorship. It is even separate from the question whether the author was literate. By oral poetry I mean poetry that reaches its audience through the medium of recitation; a manuscript in the background would not alter its oral character so long as this manuscript was prompt-copy for a reciter and not a book to be sold to the public or given to the patron. The real question is whether the Homeric poems were composed for recitation. Both of them are admittedly too long to be recited as wholes. But we see from the *Odyssey* how that could be got over; a poet, asked for the story of the Trojan Horse, begins 'at the point when the Greeks sailed away' (VIII, 500); in other words, he seems to be familiar with the practice of serial or selective recitation from a poem (or body of poetry) too long to recite in its entirety. And we know that Homer was in fact thus serially recited by relays of rhapsodists at the festival of the Panathenaea, in the historical period. There is therefore no evidence that it is *not* oral, and strong probability that it is. About *Beowulf* there is no external evidence either way. It is easily recitable, and would take perhaps three hours; this, with a break in the middle, would not be too long. But about *Beowulf,* and about the Homeric poems, there is internal evidence. They both have the oral *technique,* the repetitions, and stylized diction of oral poetry. If not oral themselves, they are at least closely modelled on work that was. And this is what mainly concerns us.

It remains to ask if they are court poetry. *Beowulf* clearly is. Its preoccupation with honour, its exclusive attention to the life of courts, its interest in etiquette (*dugupe peaw*) and in genealogy, put the matter beyond doubt. Homer is more doubtful. We have seen that in historical times it was recited not in courts, but at great national festivals, and it is possible that it was also composed for these. In other words, it is either court-poetry or festival poetry. If it is the latter, then epic, since the time of the earliest lays, has moved up, not down. The original *solemnity* of the hall has been replaced by the greater *solemnity* of the temple or the forum. Our first picture of the epic poet needs to be modified by the associations of incense, sacrifice, civic pride, and public holiday; and since this change certainly occurred sooner or later we may as well make the adjustment now. We move a stage *further away* from the solitary, private, and armchair associations which the word 'poetry' has for a modern.

Homer and *Beowulf*, then, however or whenever they were actually produced, are in the tradition of Primary epic, and inherit both its oral technique and its festal, aristocratic, public, ceremonial tone. The aesthetic consequences of this now claim our attention.

4

THE TECHNIQUE OF PRIMARY EPIC

> And the words of his mouth were as slaves spreading carpets of glory Embroidered with names of the Djinns—a miraculous weaving— But the cool and perspicuous eye overbore unbelieving.
>
> —KIPLING.

The most obvious characteristic of an oral technique is its continual use of stock words, phrases, or even whole lines. It is important to realize at the outset that these are not a second-best on which the poets fall back when inspiration fails them: they are as frequent in the great passages as in the low ones. In 103 lines of the parting between Hector and Andromache (justly regarded as one of the peaks of European poetry) phrases, or whole lines, which occur again and again in Homer are twenty-eight times employed (*Il.* VI, 390-493). Roughly speaking, a *quarter* of the whole passage is 'stock.' In Beowulf's last speech to Wiglaf (*Beow.* 2794-820) 'stock' expressions occur six times in twenty-eight lines—again, they are about a quarter of the whole.

This phenomenon has been explained often enough from the poet's side. 'These repetitions,' says Mr. Nilsson, 'are a great aid for the singer for whilst reciting them mechanically he is subconsciously forming the next verse' (*Homer and Mycenae,* 203). But all art is made to *face* the audience. Nothing can be left exposed, however useful to the performer, which is not delightful or at least tolerable to *them.* A stage set must be judged from in front. If the poet's ease were the sole consideration, why have a recitation at all? Is he not very well already, with his wine at his elbow and his share in the roast pork? We must therefore consider what these repetitions do for the hearers, not what they do for the poet. And we may observe that this is the only *aesthetic* or critical question. Music means not the noises it is nice to make, but the noises it is nice to hear. Good poetry means not the poetry men like composing, but the poetry men like to listen to or to read.

If any one will make the experiment for a week or two of reading no poetry and hearing a good deal, he will soon find the explanation of the stock phrases. It is a prime necessity of oral poetry that the hearers should not be surprised too often, or too much. The unexpected tires us: it also takes us longer to understand and enjoy than the expected. A line which gives the listener pause is a disaster in oral poetry because it makes him lose the next line. And even if he does not lose the next, the rare and ebullient line is not worth making. In the sweep of recitation *no* individual line is going to count for very much. The pleasure which moderns chiefly desire from printed poetry is ruled out anyway. You cannot ponder over single lines and let them dissolve on the mind like lozenges. That is the wrong way of using this sort of poetry. It is not built up of isolated effects; the poetry is in the paragraph, or the whole episode. To look for single, 'good' lines is like looking for single 'good' stones in a cathedral.

The language, therefore, must be *familiar* in the sense of being expected. But in Epic which is the highest species of oral court poetry, it must not be *familiar* in the sense of being colloquial or commonplace. The desire for simplicity is a late and sophisticated one. We moderns may like dances which are hardly distinguishable from walking and poetry which sounds as if it might be uttered *ex tempore*. Our ancestors did not. They liked a dance which *was* a dance, and fine clothes which no one could mistake for working clothes, and feasts that no one could mistake for ordinary dinners, and poetry that unblushingly proclaimed itself to be poetry. What is the point of having a poet, inspired by the Muse, if he tells the stories just as you or I would have told them? It will be seen that these two demands, taken together, absolutely necessitate a Poetic Diction; that is, a language which is familiar because it is used in every part of every poem, but unfamiliar because it is not used outside poetry. A parallel, from a different sphere, would be turkey and plum pudding on Christmas day; no one is surprised at the menu, but every one recognizes that it is not *ordinary* fare. Another parallel would be the language of a liturgy. Regular church-goers are not surprised by the service—indeed, they know a good deal of it by rote; but it is a language apart. Epic diction, Christmas fare, and the liturgy, are all examples of ritual—that is, of something set deliberately apart from daily usage, but wholly familiar within its own sphere. The element of ritual which some dislike in Milton's poetry thus comes into epic at the very beginning. Its propriety in Milton will be considered later; but those who dislike ritual in general—ritual in any and every department of life—may be asked most earnestly to reconsider the question. It is a pattern imposed on the mere flux of our feelings by reason and will, which renders pleasures less fugitive and griefs more endurable, which hands over to the power of wise custom the task (to which the individual and his moods are so inadequate) of being festive or sober, gay or reverent, when we choose to be, and not at the bidding of chance.

This is the common ground of all oral poetry. Against it we can now discern differences between one poem and another. The epic diction of Homer is not the same as that of *Beowulf.* It seems to me almost certain, from the language and metre, that the Greek epic was recited more quickly. It therefore needs more, and more complete, repetition.

The actual operation of the Homeric diction is remarkable. The unchanging recurrence of his *wine-dark sea,* his *rosy-fingered dawn,* his ships launched *into the holy brine,* his *Poseidon shaker of earth,* produce an effect which modern poetry, except where it has learned from Homer himself, cannot attain. They emphasize the unchanging human environment. They express a feeling very profound and very frequent in real life, but elsewhere ill represented in literature. What is really in our minds when we first catch sight of the sea after a long absence, or look up, as watchers in a sickroom or as sentries, to see yet another daybreak? Many things, no doubt—all manner of hopes and fears, pain or pleasure, and the beauty or grimness of that particular sea and that particular dawn. Yes; but under all these, like a base so deep as to be scarcely audible, there is something which we might very lamely express by muttering 'same old sea' or 'same old morning.' The permanence, the indifference, the heartrending or consoling fact that whether we laugh or weep the world is what it is, always enters into our experience and plays no small part in that pressure of reality which is one of the differences between life and imagined life. But in Homer the pressure is there. The sonorous syllables in which he has stereotyped the sea, the gods, the morning, or the mountains, make it appear that we are dealing not with poetry about the things, but almost with the things themselves. It is this that produces what Kinglake (*Eothen,* cap. IV) called 'the strong vertical light of Homer's poetry' and made Mr. Barfield say that in it 'not man was creating, but the gods' (*Poetic Diction,* 96).

The general result of this is that Homer's poetry is, in an unusual degree, believable. There is no use in disputing whether any episode could really have happened. We have seen it happen—and there seemed to be no poet mediating between us and the event. A girl walks on the shore and an unknown lover embraces her, and a darkly shining wave arched over them like a coverlet while they lay; and when he had ended his deeds of love, he told his name, 'Lo, I am Poseidon, shaker of earth' (*Od.* XI, 242-52). Because we have had 'shaker of earth' time and again in these poems where no miracle was involved, because those syllables have come to affect us almost as the presence of the unchanging sea in the real world, we are compelled to accept this. Call it nonsense, if you will; we have seen it. The real salt sea itself, and not any pantomime or Ovidian personage living *in* the sea, has got a mortal woman with child. Scientists and theologians must explain it as best they can. The *fact* is not disputable.

The diction also produces the unwearying splendour and ruthless poignancy of the Homeric poems. Miserable or even sordid events may happen; but the brightness of the sun, the 'leaf-shaking' largeness of the mountains, the steady strength of rivers, is there all the time, not with any suggestion (as it might be in a romantic poet) of the 'consolations of nature' but simply as a fact. Homeric splendour is the splendour of

reality. Homeric pathos strikes hard precisely because it seems unintended and inevitable like the pathos of real life. It comes from the clash between human emotions and the large, indifferent background which the conventional epithets represent. Ὣς φάτο, τοὺς δ' ἤδη κάτεχεν φυσίζοος αἶα. (*Il.* III, 243). Thus Helen spoke about her brothers, thinking them alive, but in fact the life-giving earth already covered them, in Lacedaemon, their dear fatherland. Ruskin's comment cannot be improved upon: 'Note here the high poetical truth carried to the extreme. The poet has to speak of the earth in sadness, but he will not let that sadness affect or change his thoughts of it. No; though Castor and Pollux be dead, yet the earth is our mother still, fruitful, life-giving. These are the facts of the thing. I see nothing else than these. Make what you will of them' (*Modern Painters*, IV, xiii, *Of the Pathetic Fallacy*). And yet even this does not quite exhaust the passage. In translating we have had to say 'their dear fatherland.' But *dear* is misleading. The word that Homer uses does not really describe any one's emotions at any particular moment. It is used whenever he mentions anything which is a man's *own*, so that a dull critic might say it was simply the Homeric Greek for *own* the adjective. But it is rather more than that. It is the word for *dear*, but by being always used comes to suggest that unalterable relation, far deeper than fondness and compatible with all changes of mood, which unites a normal man to his wife, his home, or his own body—the tie of a mutual 'belonging' which is there even when he dislikes them.

We must avoid an error which Ruskin's words might suggest. We must not think of Homer calculating these effects, line by line, as a modern poet might do. Once the diction has been established it works of itself. Almost anything the poet wants to say, has only to be turned into this orthodox and ready-made diction and it becomes poetry. 'Whatever Miss T. eats turns into Miss T.' The epic diction, as Goethe said, is 'a language which does your thinking and your poetizing for you' (*Eine Sprache die für dich dichtet und denkt*). The conscious artistry of the poet is thus set free to devote itself wholly to the large-scale problems—construction, character drawing, invention; his *verbal* poetics have become a habit, like grammar or articulation. I have avoided using such words as *automatic* or *mechanical* which carry a false suggestion. A machine is made out of inorganic materials and exploits some non-human power, such as gravitation, or the force of steam. But every single Homeric phrase was originally invented by a man and is, like all language, a human thing. It is like a machine insofar as the individual poet liberates, by using it, power other than his own; but it is stored human life and human experience which he is liberating—not *his own* life and experience, but none-the-less human and spiritual. The picture of a Muse—a superpersonal figure, yet anthropomorphically conceived—is therefore really more *accurate* than that of some kind of engine. No doubt all this is very unlike the recipe for poetry which finds favour today. But there is no fighting against facts. Make what you can of it, the result of this wholly artificial diction is a degree of objectivity which no other poetry has ever surpassed. Homer accepts artificiality from the outset: but in the result he is something for which 'natural' is too weak an epithet. He has no more need to bother about being 'natural' than Nature herself.

To a limited extent the technique of *Beowulf* is the same as that of Homer. It, too, has its reiterated expressions, *under wolcnum, in geardum,* and the like, and its 'poetical' names for most of the things the author wants to mention. One of its differences from Homer, indeed, is the number of synonymous words which the poet can use for the same thing: Homer has no list of alternatives to compare to the Beowulfian words for man—*beorn, freca, guma, hælep, secg, wer.* In the same way, Beowulf is fonder than Homer of partial repetition, of using slightly varied forms of a poetic phrase or compound. Thus, from the passage already mentioned, *Wuldorcyninge* does not, I think, occur elsewhere in the poem, but *wuldres wealdend* and *wuldres hyrde* do. *Wordum secge* is similarly a partial repetition of *wordum bædon, wordum wrixlan,* and *wordum nægde; wyrd forsweop,* of *wyrd fornam, deap fornam,* and *gupdeap fornam.* In part, this difference of technique goes with a shorter line, a language more full of consonants, and doubtless a slower and more emphatic delivery. It goes with the difference between a quantitative metre and one which uses both quantity and stress accent, demanding their union for that characteristic of alliterative verse which is called weight. One of Homer's great passages is like a cavalry charge; one of *Beowulf*'s, like blows from a hammer or the repeated thunder of breakers on the beach. The words flow in Homer; in *Beowulf* they fall apart into massive lumps. The audience has more time to chew on them. Less help is needed from pure reiteration.

All this is not unconnected with a deeper difference of temper. The objectivity of the unchanging background which is the glory of Homer's poetry, is not equally a characteristic of *Beowulf*. Compared with the *Iliad*, *Beowulf* is already, in one sense, 'romantic.' Its landscapes have a spiritual quality. The country which Grendel haunts expresses the same things as Grendel himself: the 'visionary dreariness' of Wordsworth is foreshadowed. Poetry has lost by the change, but it has gained, too. The Homeric Cyclops is a mere puppet beside the sad, excluded *ellorgast*, or the jealous and joyless dragon, of the English poem. There is certainly not more suffering behind *Beowulf* than there is behind the *Iliad*; but there is a consciousness of good and evil which Homer lacks.

The 'proper' oral technique of the later poem, that which distinguishes it most sharply from Homer, is the variation or parallelism which most of us have first met in the Psalms. 'He that dwelleth in heaven shall laugh them to scorn; the Lord shall have them in derision.' The rule is that nearly everything must be said more than once. The cold prose about the ship in which Scyld's dead body was sent away (*Beow.*, 50) is that nobody knew what became of it. The poetical rendering is that 'Men know not to say for a truth, the talkers in the hall know not, warriors under the sky know not, who received that cargo.'

5

The Subject of Primary Epic

> The Gods made a man called Kvásir who was so wise you couldn't ask him any question he hadn't got an answer to. He travelled all over the world teaching men things, until he became the guest of two dwarfs. They got him talking and managed to kill him. Then they mixed honey with his blood and made such a mead of it that anybody who drinks it becomes a poet.
>
> —*Abridged from Bragaröpur,* LVII.

In the foregoing account of Primary Epic the reader may have noticed that no mention is made of one characteristic which later critics have sometimes thought essential. Nothing has been said about greatness of subject. No doubt, the epics we have been considering do not deal with comic or idyllic matters; but what of the epic theme as later ages have conceived it—the large national or cosmic subject of super-personal interest?

In my opinion the great subject ('the life of Arthur, or Jerusalem's fall') was not a mark of primary epic. It enters the epic with Virgil, whose position in this story is central and who has altered the very notion of epic; so much so that I believe we are now tempted to read the great subject into primary epic where it does not exist. But since this may be disputed, let us consider *Beowulf* and the Homeric poems from this point of view.

The *Odyssey* is clearly out of the running. The mere fact that these adventures happened to Odysseus while he was returning from the Trojan War does not make that war the subject of the poem. Our interest is in the fortunes of an individual. If he is a king, he is the king of a very small country, and there is hardly any attempt to make Ithaca seem important, save as the hero's home and estate are important in any story. There is no pretence, indeed no possibility of pretending, that the world, or even Greece, would have been much altered if Odysseus had never got home at all. The poem is an adventure story. As far as greatness of subject goes, it is much closer to *Tom Jones* or *Ivanhoe* than to the *Aeneid* or the *Gierusalemme Liberata.*

For the *Iliad* a much more plausible case could be made out. It has been treated as an epic about the clash between East and West; and even in ancient times Isocrates praised Homer for celebrating those who fought against the 'Barbarian.' Professor Murray to some extent favours this view. It is perhaps presumptuous of me to differ from so great a scholar; and it is certainly disagreeable to differ from one whose books, eagerly read in my teens, are now in my very bones, and whose lectures are still among the most rapturous memories of my undergraduate days. But on this matter I cannot go with him. Professor Murray asks of the *Iliad,* 'Is it not the story of the battle of All-Greeks against the barbarian of Asia? "All-Greeks": the wonderful word rings out again and again in the poems.'[1] This is not the impression I get. If we examine the nine places where the index of the Oxford *Iliad* mentions the word Ραναχαιῶν as occurring (and four of them occur in a single book) we find that on eight of the occasions it is preceded by ἀριστῆες or ἀριστῆας—'the champions of the Panachaeoi.' There is no contrast suggested between the All-Greeks and the Barbarians; only between the All-Greeks, the Greeks as a whole, and their own best men. In the ninth passage (IX, 301) Odysseus bids Achilles, even if he hates Agamemnon, to pity the other All-Greeks. Here again, the 'All' seems to point a contrast between the totality of the Greeks and one member of that totality: there is no idea, so far as I can see, of the Greeks united against the Barbarians. One begins to wonder whether the first syllable of õαναχαιῶν is much more than a metrical convenience.

When I survey the poem as a whole I am even less convinced. The Trojan War is not the subject of the *Iliad.* It is

1. *Rise of the Greek Epic,* 211.

merely the background to a purely personal story—that of Achilles' wrath, suffering, repentance, and killing of Hector. About the fall of Troy, Homer has nothing to say, save incidentally. It has been argued that he does not need to, because the fall of Troy was inevitable after Hector's death; but it is, to me, hardly credible that the climax of a story—and the fall would be the climax if the siege were the theme—should be left to be inferred. At best, it would be an extreme subtlety; the art of Kipling rather than of Homer. Nor do I find any anti-Trojan feeling in the *Iliad*. The noblest character is a Trojan, and nearly all the atrocities are on the Greek side. I find even no hint (except possibly in III, 2-9) that the Trojans are regarded, either for better or for worse, as being a different *kind* of people from the Greeks. No doubt it is possible to suppose an earlier version in which the Trojans *were* hated—just as it is possible to suppose an earlier *Beowulf* free from all the Christian passages, or a 'historical' Jesus totally different from the figure in the Synoptic tradition. But that, I confess, is a mode of 'research' I heartily distrust. 'Entities are not to be feigned without necessity,' and there is no necessity here. Parallels from other literatures suggest that Primary Epic simply wants a heroic story and cares nothing about a 'great national subject.' Professor Chadwick, speaking of the Germanic epics, remarks 'how singularly free the poems are from anything in the nature of national interest or sentiment.'[2] The greatest hero of Icelandic poetry is a Burgundian. In *Beowulf* Professor Chadwick's statement is very well illustrated. The poem is English. The scene is at first laid in Zealand, and the hero comes from Sweden. Hengest, who ought to have been the Aeneas of our epic if the poet had had Virgil's notion of an epic subject, is mentioned only parenthetically.

The truth is that Primary Epic neither had, nor could have, a great subject in the later sense. That kind of greatness arises only when some event can be held to effect a profound and more or less permanent change in the history of the world, as the founding of Rome did, or still more, the fall of man. Before any event can have that significance, history must have some degree of pattern, some design. The mere endless up and down, the constant aimless alternations of

2. *The Heroic Age*, 34.

glory and misery, which make up the terrible phenomenon called a Heroic Age, admit no such design. No one event is really very much more important than another. No achievement can be permanent: today we kill and feast, tomorrow we are killed, and our women led away as slaves. Nothing 'stays put,' nothing has a significance beyond the moment. Heroism and tragedy there are in plenty, therefore good stories in plenty; but no 'large design that brings the world out of the good to ill.' The total effect is not a pattern, but a kaleidoscope. If Troy falls, woe to the Trojans, no doubt, but what of it? 'Zeus has loosened the heads of many cities, and many more will he loosen yet' (*Il.* IX, 25). Heorot has been built nobly, but in the end what of it ? From the very outset, 'High, horn-gabled, the hall rises, Waits the welter of war's surges, And the fire, its foe' (*Beow.*, 81).

Much has been talked of the melancholy of Virgil; but an inch beneath the bright surface of Homer we find not melancholy but despair. 'Hell' was the word Goethe used of it. It is all the more terrible because the poet takes it all for granted, makes no complaint. It comes out casually, in similes.

> As when the smoke ascends to the sky from a city afar
> Set in an isle, which foes have compassed round in war,
> And all day long they struggle as hateful Ares bids.
>
> (*Il.* XVIII, 207)

Or again,

> As when a woman upon the body falls
> Of her husband, killed in battle before the city walls...
> She sees him down and listens how he gasps his life away,
> And clings to the body, crying, amid the foes; but they
> Beating her back and shoulders with butts of spears amain
> Pull her away to slavery to learn of toil and pain.
>
> (*Od.* VIII, 523)

Notice how different this is from the sack of Troy in *Aeneid* II. This is a mere simile—the sort of thing that happens every day. The fall of Virgil's Troy is a catastrophe, the end of an epoch. *Urbs antiqua ruit*—'an ancient city, empress of long ages, falls.' For Homer it is all in the day's work. *Beowulf* strikes the same note. Once the king is dead, we know what is in store for us: that little island of happiness, like many another before it and many another in the years that follow, is submerged, and the great tide of the Heroic Age rolls over it:

> Laughter has left us with our Lord's slaying,
> And mirth and music. Many a spearshaft
> Shall freeze our fingers in frightened dawn,
> As our hands hold it. No harp's delight
> Shall waken warriors. The wan raven
> Keen for carrion, his call sending,
> Shall utter to the eagle how he ate his fill
> At War's banquet; the wolf shared it.
>
> (*Beow.*, 3020)

Primary Epic is great, but not with the greatness of the later kind. In Homer, its greatness lies in the human and personal tragedy built up against this background of meaningless flux. It is all the more tragic because there hangs over the heroic world a certain futility. 'And here I sit in Troy,' says Achilles to Priam, 'afflicting you and your children.' Not 'protecting Greece,' not even 'winning glory,' not called by any vocation to afflict Priam, but just doing it because that is the way things come about. We are in a different world here from Virgil's *mens immota manet.* There the suffering has a meaning, and is the price of a high resolve. Here there is just the suffering. Perhaps this was in Goethe's mind when he said, 'The lesson of the *Iliad* is that on this earth we must enact Hell.' Only the style—the unwearying, unmoved, angelic speech of Homer—makes it endurable. Without that the *Iliad* would be a poem beside which the grimmest modern realism is child's play.

Beowulf is a little different. In Homer the background of accepted, matter-of-fact despair is, after all, a background. In *Beowulf* that fundamental darkness comes out into the foreground and is partly embodied in the monsters. And against those monsters the hero fights. No one in Homer had fought against the darkness. In the English poem we have the characteristic theme of Northern mythology—the gods and men ranged in battle against the giants. To that extent the poem is more cheerful at heart, though not on the surface, and has the first hint of the Great Subject. In this way, as in several others, it stands between the *Iliad* and Virgil. But it does not approach Virgil very closely. The monsters only partly embody the darkness. Their defeat—or its defeat in them—is not permanent or even long lasting. Like every other Primary Epic it leaves matters much as it found them: the Heroic Age is still going on at the end.

6

Virgil and the Subject of Secondary Epic

This visage tells thee that my doom is past;
Nor should the change be mourned, even if the joys
Of sense were able to return as fast
And surely as they vanish. Earth destroys
Those raptures duly—Erebus disdains:
Calm pleasures there abide—majestic pains.

—*WORDSWORTH.*

The epic subject, as later critics came to understand it, is Virgil's invention; he has altered the very meaning of the word epic. Starting from the desire that the Romans should have a great poem to rival the *Iliad,* he had to ask himself what kind of poem would really express and satisfy the Roman spirit. The answer to this question he doubtless found in his own heart; we can find it by considering the earlier Roman attempts in this kind. The two previous Latin epics had been quite remarkably unlike Homer. Naevius had told the story of the first Punic War, but apparently on so large a scale that he could begin with the legend of Aeneas. Ennius, starting with the same legend, had worked steadily through the history of his people down to his own time. It is clear that both poets wrote what we should call metrical chronicles, things very much more like the work of Layamon and Robert of Gloucester than that of Homer. They catered for a taste common to the Romans and ourselves, but curiously lacking among the Greeks. Neither Herodotus nor Thucydides attempted to trace the history of even a single Greek state from its origins. The phenomena of growth, the slow process by which some great thing has taken its present shape, does not seem to have interested the Greeks. Their heart's desire was the timeless, the unchangeable, and they saw time as mere flux. But the Romans were different. Whether directly or (as Dr. Tillyard would say) 'obliquely' their great poem, unless it was to be a mere pastiche of Homer, would have to deal with the same sort of material as Naevius and Ennius. Yet, on the other hand, so true an artist as Virgil could not be content with the clumsiness and monotony of a mere chronicle. His solution of the problem—one of the most important revolutions in the history of poetry—was to take one single national legend and treat it in such a way that we feel the vaster theme to be somehow implicit in it. He has to tell a comparatively short story and give us the illusion of having lived through a great space of time. He has to deal with a limited number of personages and make us feel as if national, or almost cosmic, issues are involved. He must locate his action in a legendary past and yet make us feel the present, and the intervening centuries, already foreshadowed. After Virgil and Milton, this procedure seems obvious enough. But it is obvious only because a great poet, faced with an all but insoluble problem, discovered this answer and with it discovered new possibilities for poetry itself.

Partly as the result of romantic primitivism a silly habit has grown up of making Homer a kind of norm by which Virgil is to be measured. But the radical differences between them begin to appear on the very first page of the *Aeneid*. The third paragraph of the poem (ll. 12-33) furnishes us with examples of nearly all the methods whereby he makes his comparatively simple fable carry the weight of so much destiny. Notice the key words. Carthage is an *ancient* city, facing the Tiber's mouth a *long way off*. He is already spreading out his story both in time and space. Juno hoped to give it *empire* of the earth, if the *fates* allow: but she has already heard a rumour that *one day (olim)* the Trojan seed will bruise it. The whole Punic War has come in. But Juno is not thinking only of the future; an *older war* is rankling in her mind—she thinks of her Argives at Troy wall, of the Judgement of Paris, 'and Ganymede exalted to immortal place.' We are not, you see, at the beginning. The story on which we are embarked fades backward into an even remoter past. The heroes whose adventures we are to follow are the *remnant (reliquias)* of some earlier order, destroyed before the curtain rose; survivors, and, as it were ghosts, hunted (and here wideness in space comes in again) *maria omnia circum*, while Juno bars them from Latium,

> Leading them far, for-wandered, over alien foam;
> So mighty was the labour of the birth of Rome.

The labour, the *moles*, is the point. These men are not fighting for their own hand like Homeric heroes; they are men with a vocation, men on whom a burden is laid.

The more obvious instances of this enlargement of Virgil's subject have, no doubt, often been noticed—the glimpses of the future in Jove's prophecy in Book I, or in the vision of Anchises, or in the shield, or again the connexion of the whole fourth Book with the Punic Wars. Perhaps the most moving of all these forward links is the visit of Aeneas to the site of Rome in Book VIII. The backward links are of equal importance in determining the poetical quality of the *Aeneid.* If I am not mistaken it is almost the first poem which carries a real sense of the 'abysm of time.' *Priscus, vetus,* and *antiquus* are key-words in Virgil. In Books VI to VIII—the true heart of the poem—we are never allowed to forget that Latium—*Lurkwood,* the hiding place of aged Saturn—has been waiting for the Trojans from the beginning of the world. The palace of King Latinus is very unlike any house in Homer: 'Awful with woods and piety of elder days,'

> Where carved in ancient cedar their old sires appear
> In order: father Italus and grey Sabine
> Bearing his hook in token how he loved the vine,
> And Saturn old and Janus with his double face.
>
> (VII, 180)

There is a poetry that reiterated readings cannot exhaust in all these early Italian scenes; in the first sight of the Tiber, the lonely prayer to that unknown river, and the long river journey on which the ships startle those hitherto unviolated forests. I do not know a better example of imagination, in the highest sense, than when Charon wonders at the Golden Bough 'so long unseen;' dark centuries of that unhistoried lower world are conjured up in half a line (VI, 409).

But Virgil uses something more subtle than mere *length* of time. Our life has bends as well as extension: moments at which we realize that we have just turned some great corner, and that everything, for better or worse, will always henceforth be different. In a sense, as we have already seen, the whole *Aeneid* is the story of just such a transition in the world-order, the shift of civilization from the East to the West, the transformation of the little remnant, the *reliquias*, of the old, into the germ of the new. Hence the sadness of farewells and the alacrity of new beginnings, so conspicuously brought together at the opening of Book III, dominate the whole poem. Sometimes the sense of *paes ofereode* is made explicit, as when the Trojans arrive at Actium and find themselves at last, beyond hope, disengaged from the Greek world, and this important moment is underlined by a change of season,

> Meanwhile the sun had rolled through the delaying year
> And icy winter, roughening the dark waves, was here.
>
> (III, 285)

Sometimes it is an infinitesimal change of language which may pass the reader's conscious mind unnoticed, but which doubtless plays its part in colouring his total experience, as when the old Aegean hatreds have slipped far enough behind for *crafty Ulysses* to become *unfortunate Ulysses*. Perhaps one of Virgil's most daring successes is the appearance of Creusa's ghost in Book II. The sad, ineffectual creature, shouldered aside by destiny, must come to prophesy the wife who will replace her and the fortunes of her husband in which she will have no share. If she were a living woman it would be inexcusable cruelty. But she is not a woman, she is a ghost, the wraith of all that which, whether regretted or unregretted, is throughout the poem drifting away, settling down, into the irrevocable past, not, as in elegiac poets, that we may luxuriate in melancholy reflections on mutability, but because the *fates of Jove* so order it, because, thus and not otherwise, some great thing comes about. Aeneas himself is mistaken for a ghost in the next book. In a sense he *is* a ghost of Troy until he becomes the father of Rome. All through the poem we are turning that corner. It is this which gives the reader of the *Aeneid* the sense of having lived through so much. No man who has once read it with full perception remains an adolescent.

This theme of the great transition is, of course, closely connected with the Virgilian sense of Vocation. Nothing separates him so sharply from Homer, and that, sometimes, in places where they are superficially most alike. Aeneas' speech encouraging his men in Book I (198) is closely modelled on Odysseus' speech in *Odyssey* XII (208). Both remind their followers that they have been in tighter places before. But Odysseus speaks simply as any captain to any crew; safety is the goal. Aeneas adds something quite un-Homeric:

> One day it will be pastime to recall this woe,
> Through all these freaks of fortune and hard straits we go
> Right onward to the promised home, the Latian earth,
> Where we shall rest and Ilium have her second birth.
>
> (I, 206)

Vicit iter durum pietas; with this conception Virgil has added a new dimension to poetry. I have read that his Aeneas, so guided by dreams and omens, is hardly the shadow of a man beside Homer's Achilles. But a man, an adult, is precisely what he is: Achilles had been little more than a passionate boy. You may, of course, prefer the poetry of spontaneous passion to the poetry of passion at war with vocation, and finally reconciled. Every man to his taste. But we must not blame the second for not being the first. With Virgil European poetry grows up. For there are certain moods in which all that had gone before seems, as it were, boys' poetry, depending both for its charm and for its limitations on a certain naivety, seen alike in its heady ecstasies and in its heady despairs, which we certainly cannot, perhaps should not, recover. *Mens immota manet*, 'the mind remains unshaken while the vain tears fall.' That is the Virgilian note. But in Homer there was nothing, in the long run, to be unshaken *about*. You were unhappy, or you were happy, and that was all. Aeneas lives in a different world; he is compelled to see something more important than happiness.

It is the nature of a vocation to appear to men in the double character of a duty and a desire, and Virgil does justice to both. The element of desire is brought out in all those passages where *the Hesperian land* is hinted, prophesied, and 'dim-discovered.' First through the lips of Hector's ghost, a land still without a name; then by Creusa's ghost, with the names *Hesperia* and *Tiber* added; then comes the all-important third Book, the reluctant yet unfaltering search for the *abiding city (mansuram urbem)*, always supposed to be so near and always in reality so distant, and our slowly increasing knowledge of it. It is our *ancient mother*—it is a *terra antiqua,* mighty in arms and rich in soil—it is quite close, but not for us who must go many miles about and make a different landfall—now it is in sight, but not the part of it we seek. This is the very portrait of a vocation: a thing that calls or beckons, that calls inexorably, yet you must strain your ears to catch the voice, that insists on being sought, yet refuses to be found.

In the human response to this we find the element of duty. On the one hand we have Aeneas, who suffers, but obeys. He has one moment of real disobedience in the fourth Book, which we read all amiss because an increased respect for woman and for the sexual relation have made the hero appear inhuman at the very moment when Virgil intends to exhibit (and for a historically minded reader does exhibit) his human weakness. But everywhere else he bears the yoke well, though with a wistful side-glance at those not called to bear it.

> Live happy! you whose story is accomplish'd. We
> Commanded, move from destiny to destiny.
> Your rest is won. You wander the wide seas no more,
> Nor seek that ever-vanishing Ausonian shore.
>
> (III, 496)

On the other hand, we have the women, who have heard the call, and lived long in painful obedience, and yet desert at last. Virgil perceives their tragedy very clearly. To follow the vocation does not mean happiness: but once it has been heard, there is no happiness for those who do not follow. They are, of course, *allowed* to stay behind. Every arrangement is made for their comfort in Sicily. The result is that agonized parting in which the Will remains suspended between two equal in-tolerables.

> 'Twixt miserable longing for the present land
> And the far realms that call them by the fates' command.
>
> (V, 656)

It will be seen that in these two lines Virgil, with no intention of allegory, has described once and for all the very quality of most human life as it is experienced by any one who has not yet risen to holiness or sunk to animality. It is not thanks to the Fourth Eclogue alone that he has become almost a great Christian poet. In making his one legend symbolical of the destiny of Rome, he has, willy-nilly, symbolized the destiny of Man. His poem is 'great' in a sense in which no poem of the same type as the *Iliad* can ever be great. The real question is whether any epic development beyond Virgil is possible. But one thing is certain. If we are to have another epic it must go on from Virgil. Any return to the *merely* heroic, any lay, however good, that tells merely of brave men fighting to save their lives or to get home or to avenge their kinsmen, will now be an anachronism. You cannot be young twice. The explicitly religious subject for any future epic has been dictated by Virgil; it is the only further development left.

7

The Style of Secondary Epic

Forms and figures of speech originally the offspring of passion, but now the adopted children of power.
—COLERIDGE.

The style of Virgil and Milton arises as the solution of a very definite problem. The Secondary epic aims at an even higher solemnity than the Primary; but it has lost all those external aids to solemnity which the Primary enjoyed. There is no robed and garlanded *aoidos*, no altar, not even a feast in a hall—only a private person reading a book in an armchair. Yet somehow or other, that private person must be made to feel that he is assisting at an august ritual, for if he does not, he will not be receptive of the true epic exhilaration. The sheer writing of the poem, therefore, must now do, of itself, what the whole occasion helped to do for Homer. The Virgilian and Miltonic style is there to compensate for—to counteract—the privacy and informality of silent reading in a man's own study. Every judgement on it which does not realize this will be inept. To blame it for being ritualistic or incantatory, for lacking intimacy or the speaking voice, is to blame it for being just what it intends to be and ought to be. It is like damning an opera or an oratorio because the personages sing instead of speaking.

In a general and obvious sense this effect is achieved by what is called the 'grandeur' or 'elevation' of the style. As far as Milton is concerned (for I am not scholar enough to analyse Virgil) this grandeur is produced mainly by three things, (1) The use of slightly unfamiliar words and constructions, including archaisms. (2) The use of proper names, not solely nor chiefly for their sound, but because they are the names of splendid, remote, terrible, voluptuous, or celebrated things. They are there to encourage a sweep of the reader's eye over the richness and variety of the world—to supply that *largior aether* which we breathe as long as the poem lasts. (3) Continued allusion to all the sources of heightened interest in our sense experience (light, darkness, storm, flowers, jewels, sexual love, and the like), but all over-topped and 'managed' with an air of magnanimous austerity. Hence comes the feeling of sensual excitement *without* surrender or relaxation, the extremely tonic, yet also extremely rich, quality of our experience while we read. But all this you might have in great poems which were not epic. What I chiefly want to point out is something else—the poet's unremitting *manipulation* of his readers—how he sweeps us along as though we were attending an actual recitation and nowhere allows us to settle down and luxuriate on any one line or paragraph. It is common to speak of Milton's style as organ music. It might be more helpful to regard the reader as the organ and Milton as the organist. It is on us he plays, if we will let him.

Consider the opening paragraph. The ostensible philosophical purpose of the poem (to justify the ways of God to Man) is here of quite secondary importance. The real function of these twenty-six lines is to give us the sensation *that some great thing is now about to begin.* If the poet succeeds in doing that sufficiently, we shall be clay in his hands for the rest of Book I and perhaps longer; for be it noted that in this kind of poetry most of the poet's battles are won in advance. And as far as I am concerned, he succeeds completely, and I think I see something of how he does it. Firstly, there is the quality of weight, produced by the fact that nearly all the lines end in long, heavy monosyllables. Secondly, there is the direct suggestion of deep spiritual preparation at two points—*O spirit who dost prefer* and *What in me is dark*. But notice how cunningly this direct suggestion of great beginnings is reinforced by allusion to the creation of the world itself (*Dove-like sat'st brooding*), and then by images of rising and lifting (*With no middle flight intends to soar...raise and support—Highth of this great argument*) and then again how creation and rising come potently together when we are reminded that Heaven and Earth *rose out of Chaos*, and how in addition to this we have that brisk, morning promise of good things to come, borrowed from Ariosto (*things unattempted yet*), and how *till one greater Man* makes us feel we are about to read an epic that spans over the whole of history with its arch. All images that can suggest a great thing beginning have been brought together and our very muscles respond as we read. But look again and you will see that the ostensible and logical connexion between these images is not exactly the same as the emotional connexion which I have been tracing. The point is important. In one respect, Milton's technique is very like that of some moderns. He throws ideas together because of those emotional relations which they have in the very recesses of our consciousness. But unlike the moderns he always provides a facade of logical connexions as well. The virtue of this is that it lulls our logical faculty to sleep and enables us to accept what we are given without question.

This distinction between the logical connexions which the poet puts on the surface and the emotional connexions whereby he really manipulates our imagination is the key to many of his similes. The Miltonic simile does not always serve to illustrate what it pretends to be illustrating. The likeness between the two things compared is often trivial, and is, indeed, required only to save the face of the logical censor. At the end of Book I the fiends are compared to elves. Smallness is the only point of resemblance. The first use of the simile is to provide contrast and relief, to refresh us by a transition from Hell to a moonlit English lane. Its second use becomes apparent when we suddenly return to where

far within
And in thir own dimensions like themselves
The great Seraphic Lords and Cherubim
In close recess and secret conclave sat,
A thousand Demy-Gods on golden seats.
(II, 796)

It is by contrast with the fairies that these councillors have grown so huge, and by contrast with the fanciful simile that the hush before their debate becomes so intense, and it is by that intensity that we are so well prepared for the opening of Book II. It would be possible to go further and to say that this simile is simply the point at which the whole purpose of transforming the fiends to dwarfish stature is achieved, and that this transformation itself has a retrospective effect on the hugeness of Pandemonium. For the logician it may appear as something 'dragged in by the heels,' but in poetry it turns out to be so bound up with the whole close of the first Book and the opening of the second that if it were omitted the wound would spread over about a hundred lines. Nearly every sentence in Milton has that power which physicists sometimes think we shall have to attribute to matter—the power of action at a distance.

Examples of this subterranean virtue (so to call it) in the Miltonic simile will easily occur to every one's memory. Paradise is compared to the field of Enna—one beautiful landscape to another (IV, 268). But, of course, the deeper value of the simile lies in the resemblance which is not explicitly noted as a resemblance at all, the fact that in both these places the young and the beautiful while gathering flowers was ravished by a dark power risen up from the underworld. A moment later Eden is compared to the *Nysician isle* and *to Mount Amara*. Unlearned readers may reassure themselves. In order to get the good out of this simile it is not at all necessary to look up these places in the notes, nor has pedantry any share in the poet's motives for selecting them. All that we need to know the poet tells us. The one was a river island and the other a high mountain, and both were *hiding places*. If only we will read on, asking no questions, the sense of Eden's secrecy, of things infinitely precious, guarded, locked up, and put away, will come out of that simile and enrich what Milton is all the time trying to evoke in each reader—the consciousness of Paradise. Sometimes, I admit, the poet goes too far and the feint of logical connexion is too outrageous to be accepted. In IV, 160-71 Milton wants to make us feel the full obscenity of Satan's presence in Eden by bringing a sudden stink of fish across the sweet smell of the flowers, and alluding to one of the most unpleasant Hebrew stories. But the pretence of logical connexion (that Satan liked the flowers of Paradise *better* than Asmodeus liked the smell of burning fish) is too strained. We feel its absurdity.

This power of manipulation is not, of course, confined to the similes. Towards the end of Book III Milton takes Satan to visit the sun. To keep on harping on heat and brightness would be no use; it would end only in that bog of superlatives which is the destination of many bad poets. But Milton makes the next hundred lines as Solar as they could possibly be. We have first (583) the picture of the sun *gently warming* the universe, and a hint of the enormous distances to which this *virtue* penetrates. Then at line 588, by means of what is not much more than a pun on the word *spot* we have Galileo's recent discovery of the sun-spots. After that we plunge into alchemy because the almost limitless powers attributed to gold in that science and the connexion of gold with the solar influence make a kind of mirror in which we can view the regal, the vivifying, the *archchemic* properties of the sun. Then, still working indirectly, Milton makes us realize the marvel of a shadowless world (614-20). After that we meet Uriel (*Fire of God*), and because the sun (as every child knew from Spenser and Ovid, if not from Pliny and Bernardus) is the *world's eye*, we are told that Uriel is one of those spirits who are God's eyes (650) and is even, in a special sense, God's singular *eye* in this material world (660) and 'the sharpest-sighted Spirit of all in Heav'n' (691). This is not, of course, the sun of modern science; but almost everything which the sun had meant to man up till Milton's day has been gathered together and the whole passage in his own phrase, 'runs potable gold.'

A great deal of what is mistaken for pedantry in Milton (we hear too often of his 'immense learning') is in reality evocation. If Heaven and Earth are ransacked for simile and allusion, this is not done for display, but in order to guide our imaginations with unobtrusive pressure into the channels where the poet wishes them to flow; and as we have already seen, the learning which a reader requires in responding to a given allusion does not equal the learning Milton needed to find it. When we have understood this it will perhaps be possible to approach that feature of Milton's style which has been most severely criticized—the Latinism of his constructions.

Continuity is an essential of the epic style. If the mere printed page is to affect us like the voice of a bard chanting in a hall, then the chant must *go on*—smoothly, irresistibly, 'upborne with indefatigable wings.' We must not be allowed to settle down at the end of each sentence. Even the fuller pause at the end of a paragraph must be felt as we feel the pause in a piece of music, where the silence is part of the music, and not as we feel the pause between one item of a concert and the next. Even between one Book and the next we must not wholly wake from the enchantment nor quite put off our festal clothes. A boat will not answer to the rudder unless it is in motion; the poet can work upon us only as long as we are kept on the move.

Roughly speaking, Milton avoids discontinuity by an avoidance of what grammarians call the simple sentence. Now, if the sort of things he was saying were at all like the things that Donne or Shakespeare say, this would be intolerably tiring. He therefore compensates for the complexity of his syntax by the simplicity of the broad imaginative effects beneath it and the perfect rightness of their sequence. For us readers, this means in fact that our receptivity can be mainly laid open to the underlying simplicity, while we have only to *play* at the complex syntax. It is not in the least necessary to go to the very bottom of these verse sentences as you go to the bottom of Hooker's sentences in prose. The general feeling (which will usually be found to be correct if you insist on analysing it) that something highly concatenated is before you, that the flow of speech does not fall apart into separate lumps, that you are following a great unflagging voice—this is enough to keep the 'weigh' on you by means of which the poet steers. Let us take an example:

> If thou beest he—but O how fall'n! how chang'd
> From him who in the happy Realms of Light
> Cloth'd with transcendent brightness didst outshine
> Myriads though bright: If he whom mutual league,
> United thoughts and counsels, equal hope
> And hazard in the Glorious Enterprise,
> Joynd with me once, now misery hath joynd
> In equal ruin: into what Pit thou seest
> From what highth fal'n.
>
> (I, 84)

This is a pretty complicated sentence. On the other hand, if you read it (and let the ghost of a chanting, not a talking, voice be in your ear) without bothering about the syntax, you receive in their most natural order all the required impressions —the lost glories of heaven, the first plotting and planning, the hopes and hazards of the actual war, and then the misery, the ruin, and the pit. But the complex syntax has not been useless. It has preserved the *cantabile*, it has enabled you to feel, even within these few lines, the enormous onward pressure of the great stream on which you are embarked. And almost any sentence in the poem will illustrate the same point.

The extremely Latin connexions between the sentences serve the same purposes, and involve, like the similes, a fair amount of illusion. A good example is *nor sometimes forget*, in III, 32. In this passage Milton is directly calling up what he indirectly suggests throughout, the figure of the great blind bard. It will, of course, be greatly enriched if the mythical blind bards of antiquity are brought to bear on us. A poet like Spenser would simply begin a new stanza with *Likewise dan Homer* or something of the sort. But that will not quite serve Milton's purpose: it is a little too like rambling, it might suggest the garrulity of an old gentleman in his chair. *Nor sometimes forget* gets him across from *Sion and the flowery brooks* to *Blind Thamyris* with an appearance of continuity, like the stylized movement by which a dancer passes from one position to another. *Yet not the more* in line 26 is another example. So are *sad task Yet argument* (IX, 13) and *Since first this subject* (IX, 25). These expressions do not represent real connexions of thought, any more than the prolonged syllables in Handel represent real pronunciation.

It must also be noticed that while Milton's Latin constructions in one way tighten up our language, in another way they make it more fluid. A fixed order of words is the price—an all but ruinous price—which English pays for being uninflected. The Miltonic constructions enable the poet to depart, in some degree, from this fixed order and thus to drop the ideas into his sentence in any order he chooses. Thus, for example,

> soft oppression seis'd
> My droused sense, untroubl'd though I thought
> I then was passing to my former state
> Insensible, and forthwith to dissolve.
>
> (VIII, 291)

The syntax is so artificial that it is ambiguous. I do not know whether *untroubled* qualifies *me* understood, or *sense*, and similar doubts arise about *insensible* and the construction of *to dissolve*. But then I don't need to know. The sequence *drowsed—untroubled—my former state—insensible—dissolve* is exactly right; the very crumbling of consciousness is before us and the fringe of syntactical mystery helps rather than hinders the effect. Thus, in another passage, I read

> Heav'n op'nd wide
> Her ever-during Gates, Harmonious sound
> On golden Hinges moving.
>
> (VII, 205)

Moving might be a transitive participle agreeing with *gates* and governing *sound*; or again the whole phrase from *harmonious* to *moving* might be an ablative absolute. The effect of the passage, however, is the same whichever we choose. An extreme modern might have attempted to reach it with

> Gates open wide. Glide
> On golden hinges...
> Moving...
> Harmonious sound.

This melting down of the ordinary units of speech, this plunge back into something more like the indivisible, flowing quality of immediate experience, Milton also achieves. But by his appearance of an extremely carpentered structure he avoids the suggestion of fever, preserves the sense of dignity, and does not irritate the mind to ask questions.

Finally, it remains to judge this style not merely as an epic style, but as a style for that particular story which Milton has chosen. I must ask the reader to bear with me while I examine it at its actual work of narration. Milton's theme leads him to deal with certain very basic images in the human mind—with the archetypal patterns, as Miss Bodkin would call them, of Heaven, Hell, Paradise, God, Devil, the Winged Warrior, the Naked Bride, the Outer Void. Whether these images come to us from real spiritual perception or from pre-natal and infantile experience confusedly remembered, is not here in question; how the poet arouses them, perfects, them, and then makes them re-act on one another in our minds is the critic's concern. I use the word 'arouses' advisedly. The naif reader thinks Milton is going to *describe* Paradise as Milton imagines it; in reality the poet knows (or behaves as if he knew) that this is useless. His own private image of the happy garden, like yours and mine, is full of irrelevant particularities—notably, of memories from the first garden he ever played in as a child. And the more thoroughly he describes those particularities the further we are getting away from the Paradisal idea as it exists in our minds, or even in his own. For it is something coming *through* the particularities, some light which transfigures them, that really counts, and if you concentrate on them you will find them turning dead and cold under your hands. The more elaborately, in *that* way, we build the temple, the more certainly we shall find, on completing it, that the God has flown. Yet Milton must *seem* to describe—you cannot just say nothing about Paradise in *Paradise Lost*. While seeming to describe his own imagination he must actually arouse ours, and arouse it not to make definite pictures, but to find again in our own depth the Paradisal light of which all explicit images are only the momentary reflection. We are his organ: when he appears to be describing Paradise he is in fact drawing out the Paradisal Stop in us. The place where he chiefly does so (IV, 131-286) is worth examination in detail.

It begins (131) *so on he fares. On* is the operative word. He is going on and on. Paradise is a long way off. At present we are approaching only its *border*. Distance means gradualness of approach. It is *now nearer* (133). Then come the obstacles; a *steep wilderness* with *hairy sides* (135). Do not overlook *hairy*. The Freudian idea that the happy garden is an image of the human body would not have frightened Milton in the least, though, of course, the main point is that the ascent was *grotesque and wild* (136) and *access denied* (137). But we want something more than obstacle. Remember that in this kind of poetry the poet's battles are mainly won in advance. If he can give us the idea of increasing expectancy, the idea of the Paradisal light coming but not yet come, then, when at last he has to make a show of describing the garden itself, we shall be already conquered. He is doing his work *now* so that when the climax comes we shall actually do the work for ourselves. Therefore, at line 137, he begins playing on the note of progression—upward progression, a vertical serialism. *Overhead is insuperable height* of trees (138). But that is not enough. The trees are ladder-like or serial trees (cedar, pine, and fir) with one traditionally eastern and triumphal tree (the palm) thrown in (139). They stand up like a stage set (140) where Milton is thinking of *silvis scaena coruscis*. They go up in tiers like a theatre (140-42). Already, while I read, I feel as if my neck ached with looking higher and higher. Then quite unexpectedly, as in dream landscapes, we find that what seemed the top is not the top. Above all these trees, *yet higher* (142) springs up the green, living wall of Paradise. And now a moment's rest from our looking upward; at a wave of the wand we are seeing the whole thing reversed—we are Adam, King of Earth, looking *down* from that green rampart into this lower world (144-45)—and, of course, when we return it seems loftier still. For even that wall was not the real top. Above the wall—yes, at last, almost beyond belief, we see for once with mortal eyes the trees of Paradise itself. In lines 147-49 we get the first bit of direct description. *Of course*, the trees have golden fruit. We always knew they would. Every myth has told us so; to ask for 'originality' at this point is stark insensibility. But we are not allowed to go on looking at them. The simile of the rainbow (150-52) is introduced, and at once our glimpse of Paradise recedes to the rainbow's end. Then the theme of serialism is picked up again—the air is growing purer every minute (153); and this idea (*Quan la douss aura venta*) at once passes into a nineteen-line exploitation of the most evocative of the senses, suddenly countered by the stench of Satan (167). Then a pause, as if after a crashing piece of orchestration, and we go back to the images of gradual approach, Satan still journeying *on* (172). Now the obstacles grow more formidable and it presently turns out (as the Trojans had found on sighting Italy) that the real entrance is *on the other side* (179). What follows is concerned with the main theme of the story and may be omitted here. We return to Paradise at 205. We are in at last, and now the poet has to do something in the way of description; well for him that the Paradise-complex in us is now thoroughly awake and that almost any particular image he gives us will be caught up and assimilated. But he does not begin with a particular image, rather with an idea—*in narrow room Nature's whole wealth.* The 'narrow room,' the sense of a small guarded place, of sweetness rolled into a ball, is essential. God had *planted* it all (210). Not created it, but planted it—an anthropomorphic God out of Ezekiel xxxi, the God of our childhood and man's, making a toy garden as *we* made them when we were children. The earliest and lowest levels are being uncovered. And all this realm was studded once with rich and ancient cities; a *pleasant soil* (214), but the mountain of Paradise, like a jewel set in gold, *far more pleasant* (215) so that an emotion stolen from the splendour of the cities now flows into our feeling of Paradise. Then come the trees, the mythical and numinous trees, and *vegetable gold* from the garden of Hesperus (217-22). Then the rivers, which like Alph plunge into darkness and rise from it through *pores* at the bidding of *kindly thirst* (228), and Paradise again reminds us of a human body; and in contrast with this organic dark we have *crisped brooks* above (237) and the hard, bright suggestions of *pearl* and *gold* (238). Finally, from line 246 to 265, we get actual description. It is all, most rightly, generalized, and it is short. A reader who dislikes this kind of poetry would possibly express his objection to Milton's Paradise by saying it contained 'all the right things'—odorous gums, golden fruit, thornless roses, murmuring falls—and would prefer something he had not expected. But the unexpected has here no place. These references to the obvious and the immemorial are there not to give us new ideas about the lost garden but to make us know that the garden is found, that we have come home at last and reached the centre of the maze—our centre, humanity's centre, not some private centre of the poet's. And they last only long enough to do so. The representation begins swelling and trembling at 264 with the nervous reiteration of *airs* in order that it may *burst* in the following lines—may flow over into a riot of mythology where we are so to speak, drenched. That is the real climax; and then, having been emparadised, we are ready at line 288 to meet at last the white, erect, severe, voluptuous forms of our first parents.

8
Defence of This Style

One hand a Mathematique Christall swayes,
Which, gathering in one line a thousand rayes
From her[1] bright eyes, *Confusion* burnes to death,
And all estates of men distinguished.
By it *Morallitie* and *Comelinesse*
Themselves in all their sightly figures dresse.
Her other hand a lawrell rod applies,
To beate back *Barbarisme* and *Avarice*,
That follow'd, eating earth and excrement
And human limbs; and would make proud ascent
To seates of gods, were *Ceremonie* slaine.

—*CHAPMAN: Hero and Leander,* III, 131.

I believe I am right in saying that the reaction of many readers to the chapter I have just finished might be expressed in the following words, 'You have described exactly what we do *not* call poetry. This manipulation of the audience which you attribute to Milton is just what distinguishes the vile art of the rhetorician and the propagandist from the disinterested activity of the poet. This evocation of stock responses to conventional situations, which you choose to call Archetypal Patterns, is the very mark of the cheap writer. This calculated pomp and grandiosity is the sheer antithesis of true poetic sincerity—a miserable attempt to appear high by mounting on stilts. In brief, we always suspected that Milton was bogus, and you have confirmed our suspicion. *Habemus confitentem reum.*' I hardly expect to convert many of those who take such a view; but it would be a mistake not to make clear that

1. Those of the goddess Ceremony.

the difference between us is essential. If these are my errors they are not errors into which I have fallen inadvertently, but the very lie in the soul. If these are my truths, then they are basic truths the loss of which means imaginative death.

First, as to Manipulation, I do not think (and no great civilization has ever thought) that the art of the rhetorician is necessarily vile. It is in itself noble, though of course, like most arts, it can be wickedly used. I do not think that Rhetoric and Poetry are distinguished by manipulation of an audience in the one and, in the other, a pure self-expression, regarded as its own end, and indifferent to any audience. Both these arts, in my opinion, definitely aim at doing something to an audience. And both do it by using language to control what already exists in our minds. The differentia of Rhetoric is that it wishes to produce in our minds some practical resolve (to condemn Warren Hastings or to declare war on Philip) and it does this by calling the passions to the aid of reason. It is honestly practised when the orator honestly believes that the thing which he calls the passions to support *is* reason, and usefully practised when this belief of his is in fact correct. It is mischievously practised when that which he summons the passions to aid is, in fact, unreason, and dishonestly practised when he himself knows that it is unreason. The proper use is lawful and necessary because, as Aristotle points out, intellect of itself 'moves nothing': the transition from thinking to doing, in nearly all men at nearly all moments, needs to be assisted by appropriate states of feeling. Because the end of rhetoric is in the world of action, the objects it deals with appear foreshortened and much of their reality is omitted. Thus the ambitions of Philip are shown only insofar as they are wicked and dangerous, because indignation and moderate fear are emotional channels through which men pass from thinking to doing. Now good poetry, if it dealt with the ambitions of Philip, would give you something much more like their total reality—what it felt like to be Philip and Philip's place in the whole system of things. Its Philip would, in fact, be more *concrete* than the Philip of the orator. That is because poetry aims at producing something more like vision than it is like action. But vision, in this sense, includes passions. Certain things, if not seen as lovely or detestable, are not being correctly seen at all. When we try to rouse some one's hate of toothache in order to persuade him to ring up the dentist, this is rhetoric; but even if there were no practical issue involved, even if we only wanted to convey the reality of toothache for some speculative purpose or for its own sake, we should still have failed if the idea produced in our friend's mind did not include the hatefulness of toothache. Toothache, with that left out, is an abstraction. Hence the awakening and moulding of the reader's or hearer's emotions is a necessary element in that vision of concrete reality which poetry hopes to produce. Very roughly, we might almost say that in Rhetoric imagination is present for the sake of passion (and, therefore, in the long run, for the sake of action), while in poetry passion is present for the sake of imagination, and therefore, in the long run, for the sake of wisdom or spiritual health—the rightness and richness of a man's total response to the world. Such rightness, of course, has a tendency to contribute indirectly to right action, besides being in itself exhilarating and tranquilizing; that is why the old critics were right enough when they said that Poetry taught by delighting, or delighted by teaching. The rival theories of Dr. Richards and Professor D.G. James are therefore perhaps not so different that we cannot recognize a point of contact. Poetry, for Dr. Richards, produces a wholesome equilibrium of our psychological attitudes. For Professor James, it presents an object of 'secondary imagination,' gives us a view of the world. But a concrete (as opposed to a purely conceptual) view of reality would in fact involve right attitudes; and the totality of right attitudes, if man is a creature at all adapted to the world he inhabits, would presumably be in wholesome equilibrium. But however this may be, Poetry certainly aims at making the reader's mind what it was not before. The idea of a poetry which exists only for the poet—a poetry which the public rather overhears than hears—is a foolish novelty in criticism. There is nothing specially admirable in talking to oneself. Indeed, it is arguable that Himself is the very audience before whom a man postures most and on whom he practises the most elaborate deceptions.

Next comes the question of Stock Responses. By a Stock Response Dr. I.A. Richards means a deliberately organized attitude which is substituted for 'the direct free play of experience.' In my opinion such deliberate organization is one of the first necessities of human life, and one of the main functions of art is to assist it. All that we describe as constancy in love or friendship, as loyalty in political life, or, in general, as perseverance—all solid virtue and stable pleasure—depends on organizing chosen attitudes and maintaining them against the eternal flux (or 'direct free play') of mere immediate experience. This Dr. Richards would not perhaps deny. But his school puts the emphasis the other way. They talk as if improvement of our responses were always required in the direction of finer discrimination and greater particularity; never as if men needed responses more normal and more traditional than they now have. To me, on the other hand, it seems that most people's responses are not 'stock' enough, and that the play of experience is too free and too direct in most of us for safety or happiness or human dignity. A number of causes may be assigned for the opposite belief: (1) The decay of Logic, resulting in an untroubled assumption that the particular is real and the universal is not. (2) A Romantic Primitivism (not shared by Dr. Richards himself) which prefers the merely natural to the elaborated, the un-willed to the willed. Hence a loss of the old conviction (once shared by Hindoo, Platonist, Stoic, Christian, and 'humanist' alike) that simple 'experience,' so far from being something venerable, is in itself mere raw material, to be mastered, shaped, and worked up by the will. (3) A confusion (arising from the fact that both are voluntary) between the organization of a response and the pretence of a response. Von Hügel says somewhere, 'I kiss my son not only because I love him, but in order that I may love him.' That is organization, and good. But you may also kiss children in order to make it *appear* that you love them. That is pretence, and bad. The distinction must not be overlooked. Sensitive critics are so tired of seeing good Stock responses aped by bad writers that when at last they meet the reality they mistake it for one more instance of posturing. They are rather like a man I knew who had seen so many bad pictures of moonlight on water that he criticized a real weir under a real moon as 'conventional.' (4) A belief (not unconnected with the doctrine of the Unchanging Human Heart which I shall discuss later) that a certain elementary rectitude of human response is 'given' by nature herself, and may be taken for granted, so that poets, secure of this basis, are free to devote themselves to the more advanced work of teaching us ever finer and finer discrimination. I believe this to be a dangerous delusion. Children like dabbling in dirt; they have to be *taught* the stock response to it. Normal sexuality, far from being a *datum*, is achieved by a long and delicate process of suggestion and adjustment which proves too difficult for some individuals and, at times, for whole societies. The Stock response to Pride, which Milton reckoned on when he delineated his Satan, has been decaying ever since the Romantic Movement began—that is one of the reasons why I am composing these lectures. The Stock response to treachery has become uncertain; only the other day I heard a respectable working man defend Lord Haw-Haw by remarking coolly (and with no hint of anger or of irony), 'You've got to remember that's how he earns his pay.' The Stock response to death has become uncertain. I have heard a man say that the only 'amusing' thing that happened while he was in hospital was the death of a patient in the same ward. The Stock response to pain has become uncertain; I have heard Mr. Eliot's comparison of evening to a patient on an operating table praised, nay gloated over, not as a striking picture of sensibility in decay, but because it was so 'pleasantly unpleasant.' Even the Stock response to pleasure cannot be depended on; I have heard a man (and a young man, too) condemn Donne's more erotic poetry because 'sex,' as he called it, always 'made him think of lysol and rubber goods.' That elementary rectitude of human response, at which we are so ready to fling the unkind epithets of 'stock,' 'crude,' 'bourgeois,' and 'conventional,' so far from being 'given' is a delicate balance of trained habits, laboriously acquired and easily lost, on the maintenance of which depend both our virtues and our pleasures and even, perhaps, the survival of our species. For though the human heart is not unchanging (nay, changes almost out of recognition in the twinkling of an eye) the laws of causation are. When poisons become fashionable they do not cease to kill.

The examples I have cited warn us that those Stock responses which we need in order to be even human are already in danger. In the light of that alarming discovery there is no need to apologize for Milton or for any other pre-Romantic poet. The older poetry, by continually insisting on certain Stock themes—as that love is sweet, death bitter, virtue lovely, and children or gardens delightful—was performing a service not only of moral and civil, but even of biological, importance. Once again, the old critics were quite right when they said that poetry 'instructed by delighting,' for poetry was formerly one of the chief means whereby each new generation learned, not to copy, but by copying to make,[2] the good Stock responses. Since poetry has abandoned that office the world has not bettered. While the moderns have been pressing forward to conquer new territories of consciousness, the old territory, in which alone man can live, has been left unguarded, and we are in danger of finding the enemy in our rear. We need most urgently to recover the lost poetic art of enriching a response without making it eccentric, and of being normal without being vulgar. Meanwhile—until that recovery is made—such poetry as Milton's is more than ever necessary to us.

There is, furthermore, a special reason why mythical poetry ought not to attempt novelty in respect of its ingredients. What it does with the ingredients may be as novel as you please. But giants, dragons, paradises, gods, and the like are themselves the expression of certain basic elements in man's spiritual experience. In that sense they are more like words—the words of a language which speaks the else unspeakable—than they are like the people and places in a novel. To give them radically new characters is not so much original as ungrammatical. That strange blend of genius and vulgarity, the film of *Snow-White,* will illustrate the point. There was good unoriginality in the drawing of the queen. She was the very archetype of all beautiful, cruel queens: the thing one expected to see, save that it was truer to type than one had dared to hope for. There was bad originality in the bloated, drunken, low comedy faces of the dwarfs. Neither the wisdom, the avarice, nor the earthiness of true dwarfs were there, but an imbecility of arbitrary invention. But in the scene where *Snow-White* wakes in the woods both the right originality and

2. 'We learn how to do things by doing the things we are learning how to do,' as Aristotle observes (*Ethics*, II, i).

the right unoriginality were used together. The good unoriginality lay in the use of small, delicate animals as comforters, in the true *märchen* style. The good originality lay in letting us at first mistake their eyes for the eyes of monsters. The whole art consists not in evoking the unexpected, but in evoking with a perfection and accuracy beyond expectation the very image that has haunted us all our lives. The marvel about Milton's Paradise or Milton's Hell is simply that they are there—that the thing has at last been done—that our dream stands before us and does not melt. Not many poets can thus draw out leviathan with a hook. Compared with this the short-lived pleasure of any novelty the poet might have inserted would be a mere kickshaw.

The charge of calculated grandiosity, of 'stilts' remains. The difficulty here is that the modern critic tends to think Milton is somehow trying to deceive. We feel the pressure of the poet on every word—the *builded* quality of the verse—and since this is the last effect most poets wish to produce today, we are in danger of supposing that Milton also would have concealed it if he could, that it is a tell-tale indication of his failure to achieve spontaneity. But does Milton want to sound spontaneous? He tells us that his verse was unpremeditated in fact and attributes this to the Muse. Perhaps it was. Perhaps by that time his own epic style had become 'a language which thinks and poetizes of itself.' But that is hardly the point. The real question is whether an air of spontaneity—an impression that this is the direct outcome of immediate personal emotion—would be in the least proper to this kind of work. I believe it would not. We should miss the all-important sense that *something out of the ordinary is being done*. Bad poets in the tradition of Donne write artfully and try to make it sound colloquial. If Milton were to practise deception, it would be the other way round. A man performing a rite is not trying to make you think that this is his natural way of walking, these the unpremeditated gestures of his own domestic life. If long usage has in fact made the ritual unconscious, he must labour to make it look deliberate, in order that we, the assistants, may feel the weight of the solemnity pressing on his shoulders as well as on our own. Anything casual or familiar in his manner is not 'sincerity' or 'spontaneity,' but impertinence. Even if his robes were not heavy in fact, they ought to *look* heavy. But there is no need to suppose any deception. Habit and devout concentration of mind, or something else for which the Muse is as good a name as any other, may well have brought it to pass that the verse of *Paradise Lost* flowed into his mind without labour; but what flowed was something stylized, remote from conversation, hierophantic. The style is not pretending to be 'natural' any more than a singer is pretending to talk.

Even the poet, when he appears in the first person within his own poem, is not to be taken as the private individual John Milton. If he were that, he would be an irrelevance. He also becomes an image—the image of the Blind Bard—and we are told about him nothing that does not help that archetypal pattern. It is his office, not his person, that is sung. It would be a gross error to regard the opening of *Samson* and the opening of Book III as giving us respectively what Milton really felt, and what he would be thought to feel, about his blindness. The real man, of course, being a man, felt many more things, and less interesting things, about it than are expressed in either. From that total experience the poet selects, for his epic and for his tragedy, what is proper to each. The impatience, the humiliation, the questionings of Providence go into *Samson* because the business of tragedy is 'by raising pity and fear, or terror, to purge the mind of those and such-like passions...with a kind of delight stirred up by reading or seeing those passions well imitated.' If he had not been blind himself, he would still (though with less knowledge to guide him) have put just those elements of a blind man's experience into the mouth of Samson: for the 'disposition of his fable' so as to 'stand best with verisimilitude and decorum' requires them. On the other hand, whatever is calm and great, whatever associations make blindness venerable—all this he selects for the opening of Book III. Sincerity and insincerity are words that have no application to either case. We want a great blind poet in the one, we want a suffering and questioning prisoner in the other. 'Decorum is the grand masterpiece.'

The grandeur which the poet assumes in his poetic capacity should not arouse hostile reactions. It is for our benefit. He makes his epic a rite so that we may share it; the more ritual it becomes, the more we are elevated to the rank of participants. Precisely because the poet appears not as a private person, but as a Hierophant or Choregus, we are summoned not to hear what one particular man thought and felt about the Fall, but to take part, under his leadership, in a great mimetic dance of all Christendom, ourselves soaring and ruining from Heaven, ourselves enacting Hell and Paradise, the Fall and the repentance.

Thus far of Milton's style on the assumption that it is in fact as remote and artificial as is thought. No part of my defence depends on questioning that assumption, for I think it ought to be remote and artificial. But it would not be honest to suppress my conviction that the degree to which it possesses these qualities has been exaggerated. Much that we think typically 'Poetic Diction' in *Paradise Lost* was nothing of the sort, and has since become Poetic Diction only because Milton used it. When he writes of *an optic glass* (I, 288) we think this is a poetical periphrasis because we are remembering Thomson or Akenside; but it seems to have been an ordinary expression in Milton's time. When we read *ruin and combustion* (I, 46) we naturally exclaim *aut Miltonus aut diabolus*! Yet the identical words are said to occur in a document of the Long Parliament. *Alchymy* (II, 517) sounds like the Miltonic vague: it is really almost a trade name. *Numerous* as applied to verse (V, 150) sounds 'poetic,' but was not. If we could read *Paradise Lost* as it really was we should see more play of muscles than we see now. But only a little more. I am defending Milton's style as a ritual style.

I think the older critics may have misled us by saying that 'admiration' or 'astonishment' is the proper response to such poetry. Certainly if 'admiration' is taken in its modern sense, the misunderstanding becomes disastrous. I should say rather that joy or exhilaration was what it produced—an overplus of robust and tranquil well-being in a total experience which contains both rapturous and painful elements. In the *Dry Salvages* Mr. Eliot speaks of 'music heard so deeply that it is not heard at all.' Only as we emerge from the mode of consciousness induced by the symphony do we begin once more to attend explicitly to the sounds which induced it. In the same way, when we are caught up into the experience which a 'grand' style communicates, we are, in a sense, no longer conscious of the style. Incense is consumed by being used. The poem kindles admirations which leave us no leisure to admire the poem. When our participation in a rite becomes perfect we think no more of ritual, but are engrossed by that *about which* the rite is performed; but afterwards we recognize that ritual was the sole method by which this concentration could be achieved. Those who in reading *Paradise Lost* find themselves forced to attend throughout to the sound and the manner have simply not discovered what this sound and this manner were intended to do. A schoolboy who reads a page of Milton by chance, for the first time, and then looks up and says, 'By gum!' not in the least knowing how the thing has worked, but only that new strength and width and brightness and zest have transformed his world, is nearer to the truth than they.

9

The Doctrine of the Unchanging Human Heart

> Men do mightily wrong themselves when they refuse to be present in all ages and neglect to see the beauty of all kingdoms.
>
> —TRAHERNE.

We have hitherto been concerned almost exclusively with the form of *Paradise Lost* and it is now time to turn to its matter. Here also the modern reader finds difficulties. Mr. Brian Hone, the cricketer and schoolmaster, once told me that he had reconciled his boys to the need we find for notes in reading Milton by pointing out how many notes Milton would need if he read a modern book. The device is a happy one. If Milton returned from the dead and did a week's reading in the literature of our own day, consider what a crop of questions he might bring you. It would carry you far afield to make him understand how *liberal, sentimental, and complacent* had become terms of disapproval, and before you had finished you would find that you had embarked on the exposition of a philosophy rather than on merely lexical questions. Now when we read *Paradise Lost* the positions are reversed. Milton is on his own ground, and it is we who must be the learners.

How are these gulfs between the ages to be dealt with by the student of poetry? A method often recommended may be called the method of The Unchanging Human Heart. According to this method the things which separate one age from another are superficial. Just as, if we stripped the armour off a medieval knight or the lace off a Caroline courtier, we should find beneath them an anatomy identical with our own, so, it is held, if we strip off from Virgil his Roman imperialism, from Sidney his code of honour, from Lucretius his Epicurean philosophy, and from all who have it their religion, we shall find the Unchanging Human Heart, and on this we are to concentrate. I held this theory myself for many years, but I have now abandoned it. I continue, of course, to admit that if you remove from people the things that make them different, what is left must be the same, and that the Human Heart will certainly appear as Unchanging if you ignore its changes. But I have come to doubt whether the study of this mere L.C.M. is the best end the student of old poetry can set before himself. If we are in search of the L.C.M. then, in every poem, we are tempted to treat as the most important those elements which belong to the L.C.M. which remain when we have finished the stripping-off process. But how if these are not really the most important elements in the actual balance of the poem we are reading? Our whole study of the poem will then become a battle between us and the author in which we are trying to twist his work into a shape he never gave it, to make him use the loud pedal where he really used the soft, to force into false prominence what he took in his stride, and to slur over what he actually threw into bold relief. The older modern reading of Dante, with its disproportionate emphasis on the *Inferno*, and, within the *Inferno*, on the episode of Paolo and Francesca, is an example of this. The common concentration on the satiric elements in Jean de Meun's continuation of the *Romance of the Rose* is another. Sometimes, too, the features to which we give this false prominence are not really manifestations of some specially Unchanging element in humanity at all, but merely those in which the long process of change has thrown up a similarity between the old author and the modern mood. We find not the Unchanging, but a fortunate resemblance to our own modification—like the Scotchman who thought the Greek infantry must be sound Presbyterians at heart because they wore kilts. Under this delusion we may be led to suppose that Virgil is specially expressive of the Unchanging Human Heart in the Dido episode or that the death of Absalom is more 'central' than the death of Abel. I do not say that even on these terms we shall not get some value out of our reading; but we must not imagine that we are appreciating the works the old writers actually wrote.

Fortunately there is a better way. Instead of stripping the knight of his armour you can try to put his armour on yourself; instead of seeing how the courtier would look without his lace, you can try to see how you would feel *with* his lace; that is, with his honour, his wit, his royalism, and his gallantries out of the *Grand Cyrus*. I had much rather know what I should feel like if I adopted the beliefs of Lucretius than how Lucretius would have felt if he had never entertained them. The possible Lucretius in myself interests me more than the possible C.S. Lewis in Lucretius. There is in G.K. Chesterton's *Avowals and Denials* a wholly admirable essay called *On Man: Heir of All the Ages*. An heir is one who inherits and 'any man who is cut off from the past...is a man most unjustly disinherited.' To enjoy our full humanity we ought, so far as is possible, to contain within us potentially at all times, and on occasion to actualize, all the modes of feeling and thinking through which man has passed. You must, so far as in you lies, become an Achaean chief while reading Homer, a medieval knight while reading Malory, and an eighteenth century Londoner while reading Johnson. Only thus will you be able to judge the work 'in the same spirit that its author writ' and to avoid chimerical criticism. It is better to study the changes in which the being of the Human Heart largely consists than to amuse ourselves with fictions about its immutability. For the truth is that when you have stripped-off what the human heart actually was in this or that culture, you are left with a miserable abstraction totally unlike the life really lived by any human being. To take an example from a simple matter, human eating, when you have abstracted all that is peculiar to the social and culinary practice of different times and places, resolves itself into the merely physical. Human love, abstracted from all the varying taboos, sentiments, and ethical discriminations which have accompanied it, resolves itself into something capable only of medical treatment, not of poetical.

Logicians will perceive that the fallacy of the Unchanging Human Heart is one more instance of the L.C.M. view of the universal—the idea that an engine is most truly an engine if it is neither driven by steam nor gas nor electricity, neither stationary nor locomotive, neither big nor small. But in reality you understand enginehood or humanity or any other universal precisely by studying all the different things it can become—by following the branches of the tree, not by cutting them off.

We must therefore turn a deaf ear to Professor Saurat when he invites us 'to study what there is of lasting originality in Milton's thought and especially to disentangle from theological rubbish the permanent and human interest' (*Milton,* 111). This is like asking us to study *Hamlet* after the 'rubbish' of the revenge code has been removed, or centipedes when free of their irrelevant legs, or Gothic architecture without the pointed arches. Milton's thought, when purged of its theology, does not exist. Our plan must be very different—to plunge right into the 'rubbish,' to see the world as if we believed it, and then, while we still hold that position in our imagination, to see what sort of a poem results.

In order to take no unfair advantage I should warn the reader that I myself am a Christian, and that some (by no means all) of the things which the atheist reader must 'try to feel as if he believed' I actually, in cold prose, do believe. But for the student of Milton my Christianity is an advantage. What would you not give to have a real, live Epicurean at your elbow while reading Lucretius?

10

MILTON AND ST. AUGUSTINE

> Maysterful mod and highe pryde,
> I hete thee, arn heterly hated here.
>
> —PEARL, 401.

Milton's version of the Fall story is substantially that of St. Augustine, which is that of the Church as a whole. By studying this version we shall learn what the story meant in general to Milton and to his contemporaries and shall thus be the more likely to avoid various false emphases to which modern readers are liable. The doctrines are as follows:

1. God created all things without exception good, and because they are good, 'No *Nature* (*i.e.* no positive reality) is bad and the word Bad denotes merely privation of good' (*De Civ. Dei,* XI, 21, 22). Hence Milton's God says of Adam, 'I made him just and right' and adds 'such I created all th' Etherial Powers' (*P.L.* III, 98). Hence the angel says 'One Almighty is from whom All things proceed.... If not depraved from good, created all Such (*i.e.* good) to perfection' (V, 469).

2. What we call bad things are good things perverted (*De Civ. Dei,* XIV, 11). This perversion arises when a conscious creature becomes more interested in itself than in God (*ibid.* XIV, 11), and wishes to exist 'on its own' (*esse in semet ipso,* XIV, 13). This is the sin of Pride. The first creature whoever committed it was Satan 'the proud angel who turned from God to himself, not wishing to be a subject, but to rejoice like a tyrant in having subjects of his own' (XIV, 11). Milton's Satan exactly conforms to this description. His prime concern is with his own dignity; he revolted because he 'thought himself impaired' (*P.L.* V, 665). He attempts to maintain that

he exists 'on his own' in the sense of not having been created by God, 'self-begot, self-raised by his own quickening power' (V, 860). He is a 'great Sultan' (I, 348) and 'monarch' (II, 467), a blend of oriental despot and Machiavellian prince (IV, 393).

3. From this doctrine of good and evil it follows: (a) That good can exist without evil, as in Milton's Heaven and Paradise, but not evil without good (*De Civ. Dei,* XIV, 11). (b) That good and bad angels have the same Nature, happy when it adheres to God and miserable when it adheres to itself (*ibid.* XII, 1). These two corollaries explain all those passages in Milton, often misunderstood, where the excellence of Satan's *Nature* is insisted on, in contrast to, and aggravation of, the perversion of his *will.* If no good (that is, no being) at all remained to be perverted, Satan would cease to exist; that is why we are told that 'his form had yet not lost All her original brightness' and still appeared as 'glory obscur'd' (*P.L.* I, 591).

4. Though God has made all creatures good He foreknows that some will voluntarily make themselves bad (*De Civ. Dei,* XIV, II) and also foreknows the good use which He will then make of their badness (*ibid.*). For as He shows His benevolence in *creating* good Natures, He shows His justice in *exploiting* evil wills. (*Sicut naturarum bonarum optimus creator, ita voluntatum malarum justissimus ordinator,* XI, 17). All this is repeatedly shown at work in the poem. God sees Satan coming to pervert man; 'and shall pervert,' He observes (III, 92). He knows that Sin and Death 'impute folly' to Him for allowing them so easily to enter the universe, but Sin and Death do not know that God 'called and drew them thither, His hell-hounds to lick up the draff and filth' (X, 620 et seq.). Sin, in pitiable ignorance, had mistaken this Divine 'calling' for 'sympathie or som connatural force' between herself and Satan (X, 246). The same doctrine is enforced in Book I when Satan lifts his head from the burning lake by 'high permission of all-ruling Heaven' (I, 212). As the angels point out, whoever tries to rebel against God produces the result opposite to his intention (VII, 613). At the end of the poem Adam is astonished at the power 'that all this good of evil shall produce' (XII, 470). This is the exact reverse of the programme Satan had envisaged in Book I, when he hoped, if God attempted any

good through him, to 'pervert that end' (164); instead he is allowed to do all the evil he wants and finds that he has produced good. Those who will not be God's sons become His tools.

5. If there had been no Fall, the human race after multiplying to its full numbers would have been promoted to angelic status (*De Civ. Dei,* XIV, 10). Milton agrees. God says men are to inhabit earth, not Heaven, 'till by degrees of merit rais'd They open to themselves at length the way' (*P.L.* VII, 157). The angel hints to Adam that 'time may come' when terrestrial bodies will 'turn all to spirit' and 'wing'd ascend' (V, 493 et seq.).

6. Satan attacked Eve rather than Adam because he knew she was less intelligent and more credulous (*De Civ. Dei,* XIV, 11). So Milton's Satan is pleased to find 'the woman, opportune to all attempts' separated from the man 'whose higher intellectual more he shuns' (*P.L.* IX, 483).

7. Adam was not deceived. He did not believe what his wife said to him to be true, but yielded because of the social bond (*socialis necessitudo*) between them (*De Civ. Dei,* XIV, 11). Milton, with a very slightly increased emphasis on the erotic, at the expense of the affectional, element in Adam's motive, almost paraphrases this—'Against his better knowledge, not deceav'd But fondly overcome with Femal charm' (*P.L.* IX, 998). But we must not exaggerate the difference. Augustine's *ab unico noluit consortio dirimi* is closely echoed in the Miltonic Adam's 'How can I live without thee, how forgoe Thy sweet Converse and Love so dearly joyn'd' (*ibid.* 908). The sudden transition whereby the Garden of Eden, never hitherto seen in the poem save as our heart's desire, becomes 'these wilde Woods forlorn' is perhaps the finest expression of apprehended parting in any poem.

8. The Fall consisted in Disobedience. All idea of a magic apple has fallen out of sight. The apple was 'not bad nor harmful except insofar as it was forbidden' and the only point of forbidding it was to instil obedience, 'which virtue in a rational creature (the emphasis is on *creature*; that which though rational, is merely a creature, not self-existent being) is, as it were, the mother and guardian of *all* virtues' (*De Civ.

Dei, XIV, 12). This is exactly the Miltonic view. The idea that the apple has any *intrinsic* importance is put into the mouths of bad characters. In Eve's dream it is a 'fruit divine,' 'fit for Gods' and 'able to make gods of Men' (V, 67 et seq.). Satan assumes that knowledge is magically contained in the apple and will pass to the eater whether those who have forbidden the eating wish or no (IX, 721 et seq.). Good characters speak quite differently. For them the apple is 'sole pledge of his obedience' (III, 95), the 'sign of our obedience' (IV, 428), the subject of a single and just command (V, 551), 'My sole command' (VIII, 329). The view that if the apple has no intrinsic magic then the breach of the prohibition becomes a small matter—in other words that the Miltonic God is making a great pother about nothing—is expressed only by Satan. 'Him by fraud I have seduc'd From his Creator, and the more to increase Your wonder, with an Apple; he thereat Offended, worth your laughter, hath giv'n up Both his beloved Man and all his World' (X, 485). St. Augustine considers the disobedience heinous precisely because obedience was so easy (*De Civ. Dei,* XIV, 12).

9. But while the Fall *consisted* in Disobedience it *resulted,* like Satan's, from Pride (*De Civ.* Dei, XIV, 13). Hence Satan approaches Eve through her Pride: first by flattery of her beauty (*P.L.* IX, 532-48) which 'should be seen...ador'd and served by Angels' and secondly (this is more important) by urging her selfhood to direct revolt against the fact of being subject to God at all. 'Why,' he asks, 'was this forbid? Why but to keep ye low and ignorant, His worshippers?' (IX, 703). This is the direct appeal to the finite creature's desire to be 'on its own, *esse in semet ipso.* At the moment of eating 'nor was godhead from her thought' (IX, 790).

10. Since the Fall consisted in man's Disobedience to his superior, it was punished by man's loss of Authority over his inferiors; that is, chiefly, over his passions and his physical organism (*De Civ. Dei,* XIV, 15). Man has called for anarchy: God lets him have it. Thus in Milton God says that man's powers are 'lapsed,' 'forfeit,' and 'enthralled' (*P.L.* III, 176). In Book IX we are told that after the Fall understanding ceased to rule and the will did not listen to understanding,

both being subjected to usurping appetite (IX, 1127 et seq.). When Reason is disobeyed 'upstart Passions catch the government' (XII, 88).

11. This Disobedience of man's organism to man is specially evident in sexuality as sexuality now is but would not have been but for the Fall (XIV, 16-19). What St. Augustine means here is, in itself, so clear and yet so open to misunderstanding if not given in full, that we must not pass it over. He means that the sexual organs are not under *direct* control from the will at all. You can clench your fist without being angry and you can be angry without clenching your fist; the modification of the hand preparatory to fighting is controlled *directly* by the will and only *indirectly,* when at all, by the Passions. But the corresponding modification of the sexual organs can neither be produced nor dismissed by mere volition.[1] This is why Milton places a scene of sexual indulgence immediately after the Fall (IX, 1017-45). He doubtless intended a contrast between this and the pictures of unfallen sexual activity in IV and VII (500-20). But he has made the unfallen already so voluptuous and kept the fallen still so poetical that the contrast is not so sharp as it ought to have been.

It is my hope that this short analysis will prevent the reader from ever raising certain questions which have, in my opinion, led critics into blind alleys. We need not ask 'What is the Apple?' It is an apple. It is not an allegory. It is an apple, just as Desdemona's handkerchief is a handkerchief. Everything hangs on it, but in itself it is of no importance. We can also dismiss that question which has so much agitated some great critics. 'What is the Fall?' The Fall is simply and solely Disobedience—doing what you have been told not to do: and it results from Pride—from being too big for your boots, forgetting your place, thinking that you are God. This is what St. Augustine thinks and what (to the best of my knowledge) the Church has always taught; this Milton states in the very first line of the first Book, this all his characters reiterate and vary from every possible point of view throughout

1. No doubt, the Saint's physiology was superficial. I take it that the involuntary salivation of the mouth in the presence of attractive food is an equally good illustration of the disobedience of our members.

the poem as if it were the subject of a fugue. Eve's arguments in favour of eating the Apple are, in themselves, reasonable enough; the answer to them consists simply in the reminder 'You mustn't. You were told not to.' 'The great moral which reigns in Milton,' said Addison, 'is the most universal and most useful that can be imagined, that Obedience to the will of God makes men happy and that Disobedience makes them miserable.' Dr. Tillyard amazes me by calling this a 'rather vague explanation' (*Milton*, 258). Dull, if you will, or platitudinous, or harsh, or jejune: but how *vague*? Has it not rather the desolating clarity and concreteness of certain classic utterances we remember from the morning of our own lives; 'Bend over'—'Go to bed'—'Write out *I must do as I am told* a hundred times'—'Do not speak with your mouth full.' How are we to account for the fact that great modern scholars have missed what is so dazzlingly simple? I think we must suppose that the real nature of the Fall and the real moral of the poem involve an idea so uninteresting or so intensely disagreeable to them that they have been under a sort of psychological necessity of passing it over and hushing it up. Milton, they feel, must have meant something more than that! And here once again, the doctrine of the unchanging human heart comes into play. If there is no God, then Milton's poem, as interpreted by Addison, has no obvious relation to real life. It is therefore necessary to sweep away the main thing Milton was writing about as a mere historical accident and to fix on quite marginal or subsidiary aspects of his work as the real core. For there can be no serious doubt that Milton meant just what Addison said: neither more, nor less, nor other than that. If you can't be interested in that, you can't be interested in *Paradise Lost*.

And how are we to be interested in that? In two ways, I think. That decreasing number of readers to whom poetry is a passion without afterthought, must just accept Milton's doctrine of obedience as they accept the inexplicable prohibitions in *Lohengrin, Cinderella,* or *Cupid and Psyche.* It is, after all, the commonest of themes; even Peter Rabbit came to grief because he *would* go into Mr. McGregor's garden. The more common sort of readers must go a longer way round. They must try by an effort of historical imagination to evoke that whole hierarchical conception of the universe to which Milton's poem belongs, and to exercise themselves in feeling as if they believed it; they must give up the 'unchanging human heart' and try instead to live through some of its real changes. To this idea of Hierarchy which deserves a book, I will now devote a chapter.

11

HIERARCHY

> The same conception of a universal order is also of fundamental importance in the religious development of India and Persia. It appears in the Rigveda...under the name of Rta or Rita. It is usually translated as Order or Right, but it is difficult to find any equivalent for it in modern English since it is at once cosmic, ritual and moral.
>
> —CHRISTOPHER DAWSON, *Progress and Religion,* cap. VI.

> Neither can your wonted valour be turned to such a baseness, as in stead of a Prince delivered unto you by so many roiall ancestors, to take the tyrannous yoke of your fellow subject.
>
> —*Arcadia* (1590), II, cap. 28.

Johnson has complained that Milton thought men made only for rebellion and women only for obedience. Others have assumed that since he was a rebel against the monarchy of the Stuarts he must also have been a rebel against the monarchy of God and secretly of the devil's party. At the very least, there is felt to be a disquieting contrast between republicanism for the earth and royalism for Heaven. In my opinion, all such opinions are false and argue a deep misunderstanding of Milton's central thought.

This thought is not peculiar to Milton. It belongs to the ancient orthodox tradition of European ethics from Aristotle to Johnson himself, and a failure to understand it entails a false criticism not only of *Paradise Lost,* but of nearly all literature before the revolutionary period. It may be called the Hierarchical conception. According to this conception degrees of value are objectively present in the universe. Everything except God has some natural superior; everything except unformed matter has some natural inferior. The goodness, happiness, and dignity of every being consists in obeying its natural superior and ruling its natural inferiors. When it fails in either part of this twofold task we have disease or monstrosity in the scheme of things until the peccant being is either destroyed or corrected. One or the other it will certainly be; for by stepping out of its place in the system (whether it step up like a rebellious angel or down like an uxorious husband) it has made the very nature of things its enemy. It cannot succeed.

Aristotle tells us that to rule and to be ruled are things according to Nature. The soul is the natural ruler of the body, the male of the female, reason of passion. Slavery is justified because some men are to other men as souls are to bodies (*Polit.* I, 5). We must not, however, suppose that the rule of master over slave or soul over body is the only kind of rule: there are as many kinds of rule as there are kinds of superiority or inferiority. Thus a man should rule his slaves despotically, his children monarchically, and his wife politically; soul should be the despot of body, but reason the constitutional king of passion (*ibid.* I, 5, 12). The justice or injustice of any given instance of rule depends wholly on the nature of the parties, not in the least on any social contract. Where the citizens are really equal then they ought to live in a republic where all rule in turn (*ibid.* I, 12; II, 2). If they are not really equal then the republican form becomes unjust (*ibid.* III, 13). The difference between a king and a tyrant does not turn exclusively on the fact that one rules mildly and the other harshly. A king is one who rules over his real, natural inferiors. He who rules permanently, without successor, over his natural equals is a tyrant—even (presumably) if he rules well. He is inordinate (*ibid.* III, 16, 17; IV, 10). Justice means equality for equals, and inequality for unequals (*ibid.* III, 9). The sort of questions we now ask—whether democracy or dictatorship is the better constitution—would be senseless to Aristotle. He would ask 'Democracy *for whom*?' 'Dictatorships *for whom*?'

Aristotle was thinking mainly of civil society. The applications of the Hierarchical conception to private, or to cosmic, life are to be sought in other writers. When Donne says 'thy love shall be my love's sphere' he has for his background the cosmic hierarchy of the Platonic theologians, specially, I think, that of Abrabanel. Every being is a conductor of superior love or *agape* to the being below it, and of inferior love or *eros* to the being above. Such is the loving inequality between the intelligence who guides a sphere and the sphere which is guided.[1] This is not metaphor. For the Renaissance thinker, not less but more than for the schoolman, the universe was packed and tingling with anthropomorphic life; its true picture is to be found in the elaborate title pages of old folios where winds blow at the corners and at the bottom dolphins spout, and the eye passes upward through cities and kings and angels to four Hebrew letters with rays darting from them at the top, which represent the ineffable Name. Hence we are only on the borderline of metaphor when Spenser's Artegall reproves the levelling giant by telling him that all things were created 'in goodly measure' and 'doe know their certaine bound,' so that hills do not 'disdaine' vallies nor vallies 'envy' hills; in virtue of the same grand Authority who causes kings to command and subjects to obey. This is for Spenser more than a fanciful analogy. The social hierarchy has the same source as the cosmic, is indeed the impression of the same seal made upon a different kind of wax.

The greatest statement of the Hierarchical conception in its double reference to civil and cosmic life is, perhaps, the speech of Ulysses in Shakespeare's *Troilus*. Its special importance lies in its clear statement of the alternative to Hierarchy. If you take 'Degree' away 'each thing meets in mere oppugnancy,' 'strength' will be lord, everything will 'include itself in power.' In other words, the modern idea that we can choose between Hierarchy and equality is, for Shakespeare's Ulysses, mere moonshine. The real alternative is tyranny; if you will not have authority you will find yourself obeying brute force.

Hierarchy is a favourite theme with Shakespeare. A failure

1. Abrabanel, *Dialoghi d'Amore*. Trans. Friedeburg-Seeley and Barnes under the title *Philosophy of Love by Leone Ebreo*. Soncino Press, 1937, 183.

to accept his notion of natural authority makes nonsense, for example, of *The Taming of the Shrew.* It drives the Poet Laureate into describing Katharina's speech of submission as 'melancholy clap-trap.' It drives modern producers into making Katharina give the audience to understand that her submission is tactical or ironical. There is not a hint of this in the lines Shakespeare has given her. If we ask what Katharina's submission forebodes, I think Shakespeare has given us his answer through the lips of Petruchio: 'Marry, peace it bodes, and love and quiet life, An awful rule and right supremacy, And, to be short, what not, that's sweet and happy?' The words, thus taken at their face value, are very startling to a modern audience; but those who cannot face such startling should not read old books. If the poet had not meant us to rejoice in the correction of Katharina he would have made her a more amiable character. He certainly would not have gone out of his way to show us, beneath the mask of her pretended hatred of men, her jealous bullying of her sister. Nor is evidence lacking from other plays to prove that Shakespeare accepted the doctrine of 'right supremacy' in its full extent. 'Headstrong liberty' (of women from men) 'is lashed with woe,' as we learn in the *Comedy of Errors.* A child is to its parent 'but as a form in wax,' says Theseus. A child attempting to argue with a father—and that father, the sage Prospero—receives for sole answer, 'What? I say, my foot my tutor?' Even *Lear* is seen in a wrong light if we do not make more than modern concessions about parental and royal authority. Even *Macbeth* becomes more intelligible if we realize that the wife's domination over the husband is a 'monstrous regiment.' It seems to me beyond doubt that Shakespeare agreed with Montaigne that 'to obey is the proper office of a rational soul.'

Now if once the conception of Hierarchy is fully grasped, we see that order can be destroyed in two ways: (1) By ruling or obeying natural equals, that is by Tyranny or Servility. (2) By failing to obey a natural superior or to rule a natural inferior—that is, by Rebellion or Remissness. And these, whether they are monstrosities of equal guilt or no, are equally monstrosities. The idea, therefore, that there is any logical inconsistency, or even any emotional disharmony, in asserting the monarchy of God and rejecting the monarchy of Charles II is a confusion. We must first inquire whether Charles II is, or is not, our natural superior. For if he is not, rebellion against him would be no departure from the hierarchical principle, but an assertion of it; we should obey God and disobey Charles for one and the same reason—just as even a modern man might obey the law and refuse to obey a gangster for one and the same reason. And lest even so very obvious a truth as this should escape his readers, Milton has made it explicit in two contrasted passages.

The first of these is the debate between Satan and Abdiel in Book V. Both parties are sound Aristotelians, but the point is that Satan is wrong about matter of fact. Satan's argument is hampered by the fact that he particularly wants to avoid equality among his own faction, and therefore has to turn aside for a moment to explain (789 et seq.) that 'Orders and Degrees Jarr not with liberty.' He is not very explicit on the subject, *et pour cause.* The passage is one of those where (rightly and indeed inevitably) an element of grim comedy is permitted. But Satan's main contention is clear. He is maintaining that the vice-regency of the Son is a tyranny in the Aristotelian sense. It is unreasonable to assume monarchy 'over such as live by right His equals' (792). Abdiel's reply is double. In the first place he denies Satan's right to criticize God's actions at all, because God is his creator. As creator He has a super-parental right of doing what He will without question—'my foot my tutor?' In the second place, granting Satan's definition of tyranny, he denies Satan's *facts*; the Son is not of the same nature as the angels and was indeed the instrument by whom they were made. Of course, if He is *not* their natural equal, 'unsucceeded power' (818) on His part (the word *unsucceeded* links the passage with Aristotle) would not be tyranny, but just rule. And this is so obvious that Satan, in attempting to reply, is reduced to the ridiculous and incoherent theory that the angels were 'self-begot' with the kindly assistance of a chimaera called 'fatal course' (858).

The other passage comes at the beginning of Book XII. We are there told how human monarchy arose. One of 'ambitious heart'—that is, one sinning Satan's own sin—became discontent with the fraternal equality which ought to prevail among natural equals. In rejecting this he was rebelling against the 'law of nature.' His 'Empire' was therefore 'tyrannous,' and his pretence to divine Right ('As from Heav'n claiming second sovrantie') was spurious. For, as Adam points out, 'fatherly displeased,' and by that *fatherly* displeasure asserting the true hierarchical principle at the very moment of condemning a tyrannous breach of it, 'Dominion absolute' was given to Man in general over Beast in general, not to one man over other men (XII, 24-70).

The rebellion of Satan and the tyranny of a Nimrod or a Charles are wrong for the same reason. Tyranny, the rule over equals as if they were inferiors, is rebellion. And equally, as Shakespeare's Ulysses saw, rebellion is tyranny. All Milton's hatred of tyranny is expressed in the poem: but the tyrant held up to our execrations is not God. It is Satan. He is the *Sultan*—a name hateful in Milton's day to all Europeans both as freemen and as Christians. He is the *chief*, the *general*, the *great Commander*. He is the Machiavellian prince who excuses his 'political realism' by 'necessity, the tyrant's plea.' His rebellion begins with talk about liberty, but very soon proceeds to 'what we more affect, Honour, Dominion, glorie, and renoune' (VI, 421). The same process is at work in Eve. Hardly has she swallowed the fruit before she wants to be 'more equal' to Adam; and hardly has she said the word 'equal' before she emends it to 'superior' (IX, 824).

Some may say that though Milton's assertion of Divine monarchy is thus logically compatible with his republicanism, yet logic is not enough. They detect an emotional disharmony in the poem: whatever the poet may *say*, he does not in their opinion, *feel* the claims of authority as he feels those of freedom. Our actual experience in reading the poem is what counts—not logical constructions which we can make about it. But then our actual experience depends not only on the poem but on the preconceptions we bring to it. It would not be surprising if we, who were mostly brought up on egalitarian or even antinomian ideas, should come to the poem with minds prepossessed in favour of Satan against God and of Eve against Adam, and then read into the poet a sympathy with those prepossessions which is not really there.

I believe this has happened, but there is a distinction to be made. It is one thing to say that Milton failed to apply the hierarchical idea to himself, and quite another to say that his belief in it was superficial. We are not 'so grossly ignorant of human nature as not to know that precept may be very sincere where practice is very imperfect.' I am willing to admit that Milton himself probably failed in the virtues of obedience and humility: and if all you mean by a disharmony in the poem is merely that the poet thought better than he lived and loved higher virtues than he had attained, then the poem is divided. But if you mean that he paid only lip service to the principle of subordination, that the dictates of his superficial and conventional conscience were, in this matter, opposed to the deepest impulses of his heart then I disagree. The Hierarchical idea is not merely stuck on to his poem at points where doctrine demands it: it is the indwelling life of the whole work, it foams or burgeons out of it at every moment.

He pictures the life of beatitude as one of order—an intricate dance, so intricate that it seems irregular precisely when its regularity is most elaborate (V, 620). He pictures his whole universe as a universe of degrees, from root to stalk, from stalk to flower, from flower to breath, from fruit to human reason (V, 480). He delights in the ceremonious interchange of unequal courtesies, with condescension (a beautiful word which we have spoiled) on the one side and reverence on the other. He shows us the Father 'with rayes direct' shining full on the Son, and the Son 'o'er his scepter bowing' as He rose (VI, 719, 746); or Adam 'not aw'd' but 'bowing low' to the 'superior Nature' when he goes out to meet the archangel, and the angel, unbow'd but gracious, delivering his speeches of salutation to the human pair (V, 359-90); or the courtesies of lower to higher angels as 'is wont in Heav'n Where honour due and reverence none neglects' (III, 737); or Adam smiling with 'superior love' on Eve's 'submissive charms' like the great Sky-Father smiling on the Earth-Mother (IV, 498); or the beasts, duteous at the call of Eve as at Circe's (IX, 521).

The significance of all this seems to me very plain. This is not the writing of a man who embraces the Hierarchical principle with reluctance, but rather of a man enchanted by it. Nor is this at all surprising. Almost everything one knows about Milton prepares us for such an enchanting and makes it certain that Hierarchy will appeal to his imagination as well as to his conscience, will perhaps reach his conscience chiefly through his imagination. He is a neat, dainty man, 'the lady of Christ's;' a fastidious man, pacing in *trim* gardens. He is a grammarian, a swordsman, a musician with a predilection for the fugue. Everything that he greatly cares about demands order, proportion, measure, and control. In poetry he considers *decorum* the grand masterpiece. In politics he is that which of all things least resembles a democrat—an aristocratic republican who thinks 'nothing more agreeable to the order of nature or more for the interest of mankind, than that the less should yield to the greater, not in numbers, but in wisdom and in virtue' (*Defensio Secunda*. Trans. Bohn. *Prose Wks.*, Vol. I, 256). And soaring far beyond the region of politics he writes, 'And certainly Discipline is not only the removal of disorder; but if any visible shape can be given to divine things, the very visible shape and image of virtue, whereby she is not only seen in the regular gestures and motions of her heavenly paces as she walks, but also makes the harmony of her voice audible to mortal ears. Yea, the angels themselves, in whom no disorder is feared, as the apostle that saw them in his rapture describes, are distinguished and quaternioned into their celestial princedoms and satrapies, according as God himself has writ his imperial decrees through the great provinces of heaven. The state also of the blessed in paradise, though never so perfect, is not therefore left without discipline, whose golden surveying reed marks out and measures every quarter and circuit of New Jerusalem.' Mark well the reason. Not because even saved souls will still be finite; not because the withdrawing of discipline is some privilege too high for creatures. No; there will be discipline in Heaven 'that our happiness may orb itself into a thousand vagancies of glory and delight, and with a kind of eccentrical equation be, as it were, an invariable planet of joy and felicity' (*Reason of Church Government*, I, cap. 1. *Prose Wks*. Bohn, Vol. II, 442). In other words, that we may be 'regular when most irregular we seem.' Those to whom this conception is meaningless should not waste their time trying to enjoy Milton. For this is perhaps the central paradox of his vision. Discipline, while the world is yet unfallen, exists for the sake of what seems its very opposite—for freedom, almost for extravagance. The pattern deep hidden in the dance, hidden so deep that shallow spectators cannot see it, alone gives beauty to the wild, free gestures that fill it, just as the decasyllabic norm gives beauty to all the licences and variations of the poet's verse. The happy soul is, like a planet, a *wandering* star; yet in that very wandering (as astronomy teaches) invariable; she is eccentric beyond all predicting, yet equable in her eccentricity. The heavenly frolic arises from an orchestra which is in tune; the rules of courtesy make perfect ease and freedom possible between those who obey them. Without sin, the universe is a Solemn Game: and there is no good game without rules. And as this passage should settle once and for all the question whether Milton loved from his heart the principle of obedience, so they should also set at rest that imaginary quarrel between the ethical and the poetic which moderns often unhappily read into the great poets. There is no distinction here. The whole man is kindled by his vision of the 'shape of virtue.' Unless we bear this in mind we shall not understand either *Comus* or *Paradise Lost*, either the *Faerie Queene* or the *Arcadia*, or the *Divine Comedy* itself. We shall be in constant danger of supposing that the poet was inculcating a rule when in fact he was enamoured of a perfection.

12

The Theology of *Paradise Lost*[1]

They laid to my charge things that I knew not.
—*PSALM XXXV,* 11.

In so far as *Paradise Lost* is Augustinian and Hierarchical it is also Catholic in the sense of basing its poetry on conceptions that have been held 'always and everywhere and by all.' This Catholic quality is so predominant that it is the first impression any unbiased reader would receive. Heretical elements exist in it, but are only discoverable by search: any criticism which forces them into the foreground is mistaken, and ignores the fact that this poem was accepted as orthodox by many generations of acute readers well grounded in theology.

Milton studies owe a great debt to Professor Saurat, but I believe that with the enthusiasm incident to a pioneer he has pressed his case too far. He tells us that 'Milton's God is far from the God of popular belief or even orthodox theology. He is no Creator external to His creation, but total and perfect Being which includes in Himself the whole of space and the whole of time' (113); '...matter is a part of God' (114). '*Paradise Lost* identifies God with the primitive, infinite abyss' (115). He is 'utterly non-manifested: as soon as action appears in the world Milton speaks of the Son and no longer of God' (117); His 'unity is incompatible...with Trinity' (116); the 'creation of the Son took place on one particular day' (119);

1. On this subject the reader should consult Professor Sewell's admirable *Study in Milton's Christian Doctrine*. To note all the minor agreements and differences between Professor Sewell's view and my own would demand more footnotes than the modest scope of the present chapter justifies.

and He is 'the sole manifestation of the Father' (120), who remains 'absolutely unknowable' (121). By creation God 'has intensified His own existence, raising to glory the good parts of Himself, casting outside…the evil parts of Himself...to drive away the evil latent in the Infinite' (133). Milton's Urania is a being called in the *Zohar* (a thirteenth-century Jewish compilation) the Third Sephira, and Milton ascribes 'a sexual character' (accompanied, it would seem, with incest) to 'acts within the bosom of divinity' (291). When he says that God is light, Milton is thinking of Fludd's *De Macrocosmi Historia* (303).

I am not quite clear how many of these doctrines Professor Saurat regards as remote from 'popular belief' or 'orthodox theology.' If a criticism of his work were my main object I should of course endeavour to make sure. For our present purpose, however, it will be possible to leave that question on one side and, simply for our own convenience, to divide the doctrines mentioned by Professor Saurat into four groups: (1) those which really occur in *Paradise Lost*, but which, so far from being heretical, are the commonplaces of Christian theology; (2) those which are heretical, but do not occur in Milton; (3) those which are heretical and occur in Milton's *De Doctrina*, but not in *Paradise Lost*; (4) those which are possibly heretical and do really occur in *Paradise Lost*.

1. Those which occur in *Paradise Lost*, but are not heretical.

(a) That the Father is non-manifested and unknowable, the Son being His sole manifestation. This is certainly in the poem and Professor Saurat rightly quotes III, 384 et seq., where we are told that the Father 'whom else no creature can behold' is made 'visible' in the Son. It merely proves that Milton had read in St. Paul that Christ 'is the image of the invisible God' (*Col.* I, 15) which God 'only hath immortality, dwelling in the light which no man can approach unto, whom no man hath seen nor can see' (I *Tim.* VI, 16).

(b) 'As soon as action appears in the World Milton speaks of the Son and no longer of God.' Insofar as this is true it means that the Son is the agent of creation. This doctrine Milton learned from St. John ('He, sc. Christ, was in the world and the world was made by Him'—I, 10); from St. Paul ('by

Him were all things created...visible and invisible,' *Col.* I, 16); and from the Nicene Creed.

(c) 'God is light' (*P.L.* III, 3). Every instructed child in Milton's time would have recognized the quotation from the first epistle of St. John (I, 5).

2. Those which are heretical, but do not occur in Milton.

(a) The doctrine of latent evil in God. The only basis for this is *P.L.* V, 117-19, where Adam tells Eve that evil 'into the mind of God or Man' may 'come and go' without being approved and 'leave no spot or blame.' Since the whole point of Adam's remark is that the approval of the will alone makes a mind evil and that the presence of evil as an object of thought does not—and since our own common sense tells us that we no more become bad by thinking of badness than we become triangular by thinking about triangles—this passage is wholly inadequate to support the astonishing doctrine attributed to Milton. It is not even certain that 'God' means more than 'a god' (for the angels are called *Gods,* with a capital letter, in III, 341).

(b) The sexual character of acts 'in the bosom of Divinity.' I see no evidence that Milton believed in anything of the sort. Professor Saurat's doctrine depends on giving a sexual meaning to the word *play* in *P.L.* VII, 10, and in a passage from *Tetrachordon.*[2] No doubt Milton may have thought—

2. *Tetrachordon,* Prose Wks., Bohn, Vol. III, 331. Professor Saurat regards the doctrine of sexuality in the Divine Life as supplying the 'meaning' of this 'terrible' passage. Oddly enough, Milton is actually arguing in defence of the *non-sexual* element in human marriage! His argument is (a) St. Augustine was wrong in thinking that God's only purpose in giving Adam a female, instead of a male, companion, was copulation. For (b) there is a 'peculiar comfort' in the society of man and woman '*beside* (*i.e.* in addition to, apart from) the genial bed;' and (c) we know from Scripture that something analogous to 'play' or 'slackening the cords' occurs even in God. That is why the 'Song of Songs' describes 'a thousand raptures...*far on the hither side of carnal enjoyment.*' If Professor Saurat's 'sexual character' of Divine acts is taken literally, the passage in *Tetrachordon* seems to me to make against him, not for him; if it means merely 'sexual' in the sense in which any social intercourse between the sexes which provides a 'slackening' or 'vacancy' from the tensions of male society is sexual then the 'terrible' passage comes down to something which would have startled no nineteenth-century vicarage.

though he talks of it less, perhaps, than any other Christian poet—that sexual love provided an analogy for, or was even a real ectype of, celestial and Divine Love. If so, he was following St. Paul on Marriage (*Eph*. V, 23 et seq.), St. John on the Bride (*Rev*. XXI, 2), several passages in the Old Testament, and a huge array of medieval poets and mystics.

(c) 'God is...Total Being which includes in Himself the whole of time.' To support this Professor Saurat quotes from *De Doctrina* that God 'knows beforehand the thoughts and actions of free agents...the foreknowledge of God is nothing but the wisdom of God or that idea He had of everything before he decreed anything.' This is nothing to the purpose. I have never heard of any Christian, any Unitarian, any Jew, any Mohammedan, or any Theist, who did not believe the same. If such a doctrine of foreknowledge implied that God contains in Himself the whole of time (whatever that may mean), then this implication would not be heretical, but common to all Theists. But I do not see any such consequence. Professor Saurat also quotes *P.L.* VII, 154 ('I in a moment will create Another World') and 176 ('Immediate are the acts of God', etc.). These passages mean that Divine Acts are not really in time, though we are compelled to imagine them as if they were—a doctrine which the reader can study in Boethius (*De Cons. Phil.* V, *Pros.* VI), St. Augustine (*De Civ. Dei,* XI, 6, 21), or Thomas Browne (*Rel. Med.* I, XI). How it should imply that God 'includes all time' except in the sense in which Shakespeare includes (*i.e.* ordains, while not entering) the dramatic time in *Hamlet,* I do not know. It is certainly not heretical. The question about space is more difficult and will be dealt with below.

3. Those which are heretical and occur in the *De Doctrina,* but not in *Paradise Lost.*

Only one doctrine falls under this heading. Milton was an Arian; that is, he disbelieved in the coeternity and equal deity of the three Persons. Milton is an honest writer. After spending Chapters II to IV of the first Book of *De Doctrina* on God, he begins cap. V 'on the Son' with prefatory remarks which make it clear that he is *now* beginning to say something unorthodox, with the implication that he has hitherto been stating common beliefs. His Arianism, insofar as it here concerns us, is stated in the words 'All these passages prove the existence of the Son before the world was made, but they conclude nothing respecting His generation from all eternity.' Professor Saurat suggests that this heresy appears in *Paradise Lost,* V, 603, when the Father announces to the angels 'This day have I begot whom I declare My onely Son.' Now if this is taken literally it means that the Son was created after the angels. But that is impossible in *Paradise Lost.* We learn in III, 390, that God *created* the angels by the agency of the Son, and Abdiel refutes Satan by making the same assertion in V, 835—to which the best answer Satan can bring is that 'we weren't there to see it being done.' The puzzle would be insoluble if Milton had not given us the solution in *De Doctrina,* I, V, where he says that 'beget,' when used of the Father in relation to the Son, has two senses, 'the one literal, with reference to the production of the Son, the other metaphorical, with reference to His exaltation' (Bohn, Prose Wks, vol. IV, 80). And it is obvious that 'This day I have begot' must mean 'This day I have exalted,' for otherwise it is inconsistent with the rest of the poem.[3] And if this is so, we must admit that Milton's Arianism is not asserted in *Paradise Lost.* The place (II, 678) where we are told that Satan feared no *created thing* except God and His Son merely illustrates the same illogical idiom which makes Eve one of her own daughters (IV, 324); if it were taken in any other way it would make the Father, as well as the Son, a 'created thing.' The expression 'of all Creation first' applied to the Son in III, 383, is a translation of St. Paul's πρωτότοκος πάσης κτίσεως (*Col.* I, 15). A writer anxious to avoid the Arian heresy might indeed have avoided Milton's translation; but we should not from this passage, nor from any passage in the whole poem, have discovered the poet's Arianism without the aid of external evidence.[4]

3. The real question between Professor Saurat and Sir Herbert Grierson on this point is whether a sense which contradicts the rest of the poet's story is more, or less, probable than one that agrees with it.

4. I do not say anything in the text about the fact that *P.L.* has so few references to the Holy Ghost, because I suppose that no reader of the poem would notice this till it had been pointed out to him or draw any theological inference from it if he did. He is mentioned in the invocation to Book I, and His operations in the Church are dealt with pretty fully in Book XII (484-530). More than this no one would have expected. The Holy Ghost is not matter for *epic* poetry. We hear very little of Him, or of the Trinity at all, in Tasso.

4. Those which are possibly heretical and do really occur in *Paradise Lost*.

(a) 'God includes the whole of Space.' The important passage is VII, 166 et seq., where the Father commands the Son to create the World. The Son is to 'bid the Deep be Heav'n and Earth.' The Deep is 'boundless' because 'I am who fill infinitude;' then come the crucial words,

nor vacuous the space
Though I incircumscrib'd myself retire
And put not forth my goodness, which is free
To act or not.

One of Professor Saurat's great contributions has been to discover the doctrine in the *Zohar* which was almost certainly present in Milton's mind when he wrote those verses. This doctrine appears to be that God is infinitely extended in space (like ether), and therefore in order to create—to make *room* for anything to exist which is not simply Himself—he must contract, or retire, His infinite essence. I do not think such an idea likely to have struck two writers independently, and I therefore allow to Professor Saurat that Milton has been influenced by the *Zohar* when he speaks of God 'retiring Himself.' It remains to define the sense in which this is heretical. To say that God is everywhere is orthodox. 'Do not I fill heaven and earth, saith the Lord' (*Jer.* XXIII, 24). But it is heresy to say that God is corporeal. If, therefore, we insist on defining (which, to the best of my belief, no Christian has ever been obliged to do) the *mode* of God's omnipresence, we must not so define it as to make God present in space in the way in which a body is present. The *Zohar* by making God present in such a way as to exclude other beings (for if He does not exclude other beings, why need He withdraw to make room for them?) would seem to commit this error. But does Milton follow it? To be true to the *Zohar* Milton's God ought to say 'The space *is* vacuous *because* I have withdrawn;' actually He says, "The space is *not* vacuous, *although* I have withdrawn.' And Milton goes on to explain that God's withdrawal consists not in a spatial retraction, but in 'not putting forth His goodness;' that is, there are parts of space over which God is not exercising His efficacy, though He is still, in some undefined mode, present in them. This may possibly fall into a quite different heresy—that of including *potentiality* in God; but it does not commit Milton to making God an extended being, like matter. Indeed, it is doubtful if the *Zohar* itself is so committed; for having said that God 'contracts His essence' it goes on to assert that He does not thereby diminish Himself. But spatial contraction of a body would involve diminution in extent. Therefore the retraction of the *Zohar* is not really an affair of space, as we understand it, at all; and not even the *Zohar*, much less Milton, can with certainty be accused of such crude picture-thinking as we at first suspect. Finally, I would draw attention to the word 'uncircumscribed.' It is not clear to what sentence in the *Zohar* Professor Saurat supposes this to correspond. But it can be paralleled in a very different author. Thomas Aquinas, in defining the mode of God's omnipresence, distinguishes three different meanings of the words 'to be in a place' (or 'in place'). A *body* is in a place in such a way as to be bounded by it, *i.e.* it occupies a place *circumscriptive*. An angel is in a place not *circumscriptive*, for it is not bounded by it, but *definitive*, because it is in that one place and *not* in any other. But God is in a place neither *circumscriptive* nor *definitive*, because He is everywhere (*Sum. Theol.* Ia. Q. LII, Art. 2). I do not suppose that Milton, who shared to the full the Philistine attitude of the Humanists to scholastic philosophy, had himself read these words, but I think it very unlikely that the conception of *circumscription* in this sense was unknown in Cambridge in his time. And if so, his use of the word *uncircumscribed* would have called up the associations of a theory of Divine omnipresence which is perfectly orthodox. Even if this is not accepted, and if *uncircumscribed* is taken to reproduce the *Zohar's* 'not that He diminished Himself,' it will still emphasize just that proviso in the *Zohar* whereby it avoids a purely spatial conception. In fine, from this highly poetical but philosophically obscure passage, the most we can draw is that Milton is perhaps following the *Zohar* where the *Zohar* is perhaps heretical.

(b) Matter is a part of God. Milton certainly rejects in *De Doctrina* I, vii, the orthodox teaching that God made the material universe 'out of nothing,' *i.e.* not out of any pre-existing raw material. He holds it to be 'an argument of supreme power and goodness that such diversified, multiform, and inexhaustible virtue' (sc. as that of matter) 'should exist and be substantially inherent in God.' Spirit, according to Milton, 'being the more excellent substance virtually and essentially contains within itself the inferior one.' It is not easy to understand this doctrine, but we may note that it does not fall into the heresy against which the doctrine of 'creation out of nothing' was intended to guard. That doctrine was directed against dualism—against the idea that God was not the sole origin of things, but found Himself from the beginning faced with something other than Himself. This Milton does not believe: if he has erred he has erred by flying too far from it, and believing that God made the world 'out of Himself.' And this view must *in a certain sense* be accepted by all Theists: in the sense that the world was modelled on an *idea* existing in God's mind, that God *invented* matter, that (*salva reverentia*) He 'thought of' matter as Dickens 'thought of' Mr. Pickwick. From that point of view it could be said that God 'contained' matter as Shakespeare 'contained' Hamlet. In fact, if Milton had been content to say that God 'virtually contains' matter, as the poet the poem or the feet swiftness, he would (I believe) have been orthodox. When he goes on to add 'essentially' he probably means something heretical (though I do not clearly understand what) and this something presumably appears in *Paradise Lost*, V, 403 and following—a fugitive colour on the poem which we detect only by the aid of external evidence from the *De Doctrina*.

Perhaps it will be useful to mention here—though it would concern me more closely if my subject were *Paradise Regained*—what Professor Saurat believes about Milton's presentation of the Redemption. Professor Saurat says (177) that the Crucifixion plays 'no noticeable part' in the poet's theology and that 'vicarious atonement is no Miltonic conception' (178). But it is precisely the scheme of vicarious atonement in its strictest Anselmic form which the Father propounds in *P.L.* III (210 et seq.) and which the Son accepts—'On Mee let thine Anger fall...account me Man' (III, 237). Michael explains the whole matter to Adam in forensic terms. Christ will save Man 'by suffering Death, The penaltie to thy transgression due' (XII, 398): 'Thy punishment Hee shall endure' (*ibid.* 404). His 'imputed' merits will save human beings (409). He will 'nail' our enemies 'to the cross' (415) and pay our 'ransom' (424). What could Milton have done, which he has not done, to forestall Professor Saurat's criticism? Even in *Paradise Regained* it is only *Eden*—not Heaven—that Christ raises in the wilderness (*Regained,* I, 7). The perfect manhood which Adam lost is there matured in conflict with Satan; in that sense Eden, or Paradise, the state of perfection, is 'regained.' But all the vicarious atonement is still to be carried out: that is why we hear so little of it in the poem. The temptation is merely 'exercise' (I, 156) and 'rudiments' (I, 157) *preparatory to* the work of redemption, and different from it in kind, because in the wilderness Christ merely conquers Satan's 'sollicitations' (I, 152) whereas in the crucifixion He conquers 'all his vast force' (I, 153). Hence at the end of the poem the Angelic chorus bid Christ 'now enter' on His true task and 'begin' to save Mankind (IV, 634). Satan's 'moral defeat' has been achieved, his actual defeat is still to come. If the analogy is allowable, Milton has described the *enfances* and knighting of the Hero, and has really made it quite clear that the dragon-slaying is not part of his subject. It may, of course, be asked why Milton did *not* write a poem on the Crucifixion. For my own part, I think the answer is that he had more sense. But why should such a question be raised? A man is not under a contract to write every poem we happen to think suitable for him.

The heresies of *Paradise Lost* thus reduce themselves to something very small and rather ambiguous. It may be objected that I have been treating the poem as a legal document, finding out what Milton's words strictly hold him to, and thrusting aside the evidence of his other works which shows us what he 'really meant' by them. And certainly if we were in pursuit of Milton's private thoughts and were valuing the poem simply for the light it threw on those, my method would be very perverse. But the words 'really meant' are ambiguous. 'What Milton really meant by the poem' may mean (a) his total thought about all the subjects mentioned in it; (b) the poem he meant (*i.e.* intended) to write, the instrument for producing a certain experience in the readers which he intended to make. When we are dealing with the second of these two we are not only entitled but obliged to rule out any effects which his words can produce only by the aid of the *De Doctrina* or the *Zohar,* for the poem is not addressed to students of either. The modern habit of writing poems which are to be understood only in the light of the poet's own reading, however idiosyncratic and accidental it may be, was quite foreign to the classical, public, and objective conceptions of poetry which Milton held. You put into your poem not whatever you happened to be interested in, but what was proper, first, to the general end of delighting and instructing the readers, and, second, to the fable and the species of composition. Decorum was the grand masterpiece. To look away from the effect which the poem might be expected to produce, and was calculated to produce, on the ordinary educated and Christian audience in Milton's time, and to consider instead all the connexions it may have had in Milton's private thinking, is like leaving the auditorium during a tragedy to hang about the wings and see what the scenery looks like from there and how the actors talk when they come off the stage. By so doing you will find out many interesting facts, but you will not be able to judge or to enjoy the tragedy. In *Paradise Lost* we are to study what the poet, with his singing robes about him, has given us. And when we study that we find that he has laid aside most of his private theological whimsies during his working hours as an epic poet. He may have been an undisciplined man; he was a very disciplined artist. Therefore, of his heresies—themselves fewer than some suppose—fewer still are paraded in *Paradise Lost.* Urania had him in hand. The *best* of Milton is in his epic: why should we labour to drag back into that noble building all the rubble which the laws of its structure, the limitations of its purpose, and the perhaps half-conscious prudence of the author, have so happily excluded from it? Must Noah *always* figure in our minds drunk and naked, never building the Ark?

Christian readers who find *Paradise Lost* unsatisfactory as a religious poem may very naturally suspect that some of its failures in this respect are not unconnected with those heretical beliefs which, from his other works, we can bring home to the author. The suspicion will not be confirmed or removed till the Day of Judgement. In the meantime the sound course is to judge the poem *on its merits*, not to pre-judge it by reading doctrinal errors into the text. And as far as doctrine goes, the poem is overwhelmingly Christian. Except for a few isolated passages it is not even specifically Protestant or Puritan. It gives the great central tradition. Emotionally it may have such and such faults; dogmatically its invitation to join in this great ritual *mimesis* of the Fall is one which all Christendom in all lands or ages can accept.

I cannot leave this part of my subject without again expressing the thanks which are due to Professor Saurat from all lovers of Milton. I believe his book to be full of wrong answers to the questions he has raised: but to have raised those questions at all, to have rescued Miltonic criticism from the drowsy praise of his 'organ music' and babble about the 'majestic rolls of proper names,' to have begun the new era in which readers take him (as he wished to be taken) seriously, was a most useful, and a highly original, piece of work. If I am right in finding very different answers to these questions, my debt to Professor Saurat is not the less. It was from him that I first learned to look for answers at all, or indeed to suspect that they were worth finding. He has made most criticism of Milton before his time look somewhat childish or dilettante; and even those of us who disagree with him are, in one sense, of his school.

13

Satan

le genti dolorosi
C'hanno perduto il ben de l'intelletto
—DANTE.

Before considering the character of Milton's Satan it may be desirable to remove an ambiguity by noticing that Jane Austen's Miss Bates could be described either as a very entertaining or a very tedious person. If we said the first, we should mean that the author's portrait of her entertains us while we read; if we said the second, we should mean that it does so by being the portrait of a person whom the other people in *Emma* find tedious and whose like we also should find tedious in real life. For it is a very old critical discovery that the imitation in art of unpleasing objects may be a pleasing imitation. In the same way, the proposition that Milton's Satan is a magnificent character may bear two senses. It may mean that Milton's presentation of him is a magnificent poetical achievement which engages the attention and excites the admiration of the reader. On the other hand, it may mean that the real being (if any) whom Milton is depicting, or any real being like Satan if there were one, or a real human being insofar as he resembles Milton's Satan, is or ought to be an object of admiration and sympathy, conscious or unconscious, on the part of the poet or his readers or both. The first, so far as I know, has never till modern times been denied; the second, never affirmed before the times of Blake and Shelley—for when Dryden said that Satan was Milton's 'hero' he meant something quite different. It is, in my opinion, wholly erroneous. In saying this I have, however, trespassed beyond the bounds of purely literary criticism. In what follows, therefore, I shall not labour directly to convert those who admire Satan, but only to make a little clearer what it is they are admiring. That Milton could not have shared their admiration will then, I hope, need no argument.

The main difficulty is that any real exposition of the Satanic character and the Satanic predicament is likely to provoke the question 'Do you, then, regard *Paradise Lost* as a comic poem?' To this I answer, No; but only those will fully understand it who see that it might have been a comic poem. Milton has chosen to treat the Satanic predicament in the epic form and has therefore subordinated the absurdity of Satan to the misery which he suffers and inflicts. Another author, Meredith, has treated it as comedy with consequent subordination of its tragic elements. But *The Egoist* remains, nonetheless, a pendant to *Paradise Lost*, and just as Meredith cannot exclude all pathos from Sir Willoughby, so Milton cannot exclude all absurdity from Satan, and does not even wish to do so. That is the explanation of the Divine laughter in *Paradise Lost* which has offended some readers. There is a real offence in it because Milton has imprudently made his Divine Persons so anthropomorphic that their laughter arouses legitimately hostile reactions in us—as though we were dealing with an ordinary conflict of wills in which the winner ought not to ridicule the loser. But it is a mistake to demand that Satan, any more than Sir Willoughby, should be able to rant and posture through the whole universe without, sooner or later, awaking the comic spirit. The whole nature of reality would have to be altered in order to give him such immunity, and it is not alterable. At that precise point where Satan or Sir Willoughby meets something real, laughter *must* arise, just as steam must when water meets fire. And no one was less likely than Milton to be ignorant of this necessity. We know from his prose works that he believed everything detestable to be, in the long run, also ridiculous; and mere Christianity commits every Christian to believing that 'the Devil is (in the long run) an ass.'

What the Satanic predicament consists in is made clear, as Mr. Williams points out, by Satan himself. On his own showing he is suffering from a 'sense of injur'd merit' (I, 98).

This is a well-known state of mind which we can all study in domestic animals, children, film-stars, politicians, or minor poets; and perhaps nearer home. Many critics have a curious partiality for it in literature, but I do not know that any one admires it in life. When it appears, unable to hurt, in a jealous dog or a spoiled child, it is usually laughed at. When it appears armed with the force of millions on the political stage, it escapes ridicule only by being more mischievous. And the cause from which the Sense of Injured Merit arose in Satan's mind—once more I follow Mr. Williams—is also clear. 'He thought himself impaired' (V, 662). He thought himself impaired because Messiah had been pronounced Head of the Angels. These are the 'wrongs' which Shelley described as 'beyond measure.' A being superior to himself in kind, by whom he himself had been created—a being far above him in the natural hierarchy—had been preferred to him in honour by an authority whose right to do so was not disputable, and in a fashion which, as Abdiel points out, constituted a compliment to the angels rather than a slight (V, 823-43). No one had in fact done anything to Satan; he was not hungry, nor over-tasked, nor removed from his place, nor shunned, nor hated—he only thought himself impaired. In the midst of a world of light and love, of song and feast and dance, he could find nothing to think of more interesting than his own prestige. And his own prestige, it must be noted, had and could have no other grounds than those which he refused to admit for the superior prestige of Messiah. Superiority in kind, or Divine appointment, or both—on what else could his own exalted position depend? Hence his revolt is entangled in contradictions from the very outset, and he cannot even raise the banner of liberty and equality without admitting in a tell-tale parenthesis that 'Orders and Degrees Jarr not with liberty' (V, 789). He wants hierarchy and does not want hierarchy. Throughout the poem he is engaged in sawing off the branch he is sitting on, not only in the quasi-political sense already indicated, but in a deeper sense still, since a creature revolting against a creator is revolting against the source of his own powers—including even his power to revolt. Hence the strife is most accurately described as 'Heav'n ruining from Heav'n' (VI, 868), for only insofar as he also is 'Heaven'—

diseased, perverted, twisted, but still a native of Heaven—does Satan exist at all. It is like the scent of a flower trying to destroy the flower. As a consequence the same rebellion which means misery for the feelings and corruption for the Will, means Nonsense for the intellect.

Mr. Williams has reminded us in unforgettable words that 'Hell is inaccurate,' and has drawn attention to the fact that Satan lies about every subject he mentions in *Paradise Lost*. But I do not know whether we can distinguish his conscious lies from the blindness which he has almost willingly imposed on himself. When, at the very beginning of his insurrection, he tells Beelzebub that Messiah is going to make a tour 'through all the Hierarchies...and give Laws' (V, 688-90) I suppose he may still know that he is lying; and similarly when he tells his followers that 'all this haste of midnight march' (V, 774) had been ordered in honour of their new 'Head.' But when in Book I he claims that the 'terror of his arm' had put God in doubt of 'his empire,' I am not quite certain. It is, of course, mere folly. There never had been any war between Satan and God, only between Satan and Michael; but it is possible that he now believes his own propaganda. When in Book X he makes to his peers the useless boast that Chaos had attempted to oppose his journey 'protesting Fate supreame' (480) he may really, by then, have persuaded himself that this was true; for far earlier in his career he has become more a Lie than a Liar, a personified self-contradiction.

This doom of Nonsense—almost, in Pope's sense, of Dulness—is brought out in two scenes. The first is his debate with Abdiel in Book V. Here Satan attempts to maintain the heresy which is at the root of his whole predicament—the doctrine that he is a self-existent being, not a derived being, a creature. Now, of course, the property of a self-existent being is that it can understand its own existence; it is *causa sui*. The quality of a created being is that it just finds itself existing, it knows not how nor why. Yet at the same time, if a creature is silly enough to try to prove that it was not created, what is more natural than for it to say, 'Well, I wasn't there to see it being done?' Yet what more futile, since in thus admitting ignorance of its own beginnings it proves that those beginnings lay outside itself? Satan falls instantly into this trap (850 et seq.)—

as indeed he cannot help doing—and produces as proof of his self-existence what is really its disproof. But even this is not Nonsense enough. Uneasily shifting on the bed of Nonsense which he has made for himself, he then throws out the happy idea that 'fatal course' really produced him, and finally, with a triumphant air, the theory that he sprouted from the soil like a vegetable. Thus, in twenty lines, the being too proud to admit derivation from God, has come to rejoice in believing that he 'just grew' like Topsy or a turnip. The second passage is his speech from the throne in Book II. The blindness here displayed reminds one of Napoleon's utterance after his fall, 'I wonder what Wellington will do now?—he will never be content to become a private citizen again.' Just as Napoleon was incapable of conceiving, I do not say the virtues, but even the temptations, of an ordinarily honest man in a tolerably stable commonwealth, so Satan in this speech shows complete inability to conceive any state of mind but the infernal. His argument assumes as axiomatic that in any world where there is any good to be envied, subjects will envy their sovereign. The only exception is Hell, for there, since there is no good to be had, the sovereign cannot have more of it, and therefore cannot be envied. Hence he concludes that the infernal monarchy has a stability which the celestial lacks. That the obedient angels might love to obey is an idea which cannot cross his mind even as a hypothesis. But even within this invincible ignorance contradiction breaks out; for Satan makes this ludicrous proposition a reason for hoping ultimate victory. He does not, apparently, notice that every approach to victory must take away the grounds on which victory is hoped. A stability based on perfect misery, and therefore diminishing with each alleviation of that misery, is held out as something likely to assist in removing the misery altogether (II, 11-43).

What we see in Satan is the horrible co-existence of a subtle and incessant intellectual activity with an incapacity to understand anything. This doom he has brought upon himself; in order to avoid seeing one thing he has, almost voluntarily, incapacitated himself from seeing at all. And thus, throughout the poem, all his torments come, in a sense, at his own bidding, and the Divine judgement might have been expressed in the words '*thy* will be done.' He says 'Evil be thou my good' (which includes 'Nonsense be thou my sense') and his prayer is granted. It is by his own will that he revolts; but not by his own will that Revolt itself tears its way in agony out of his head and becomes a being separable from himself, capable of enchanting him (II, 749-66) and bearing him unexpected and unwelcome progeny. By his own will he becomes a serpent in Book IX; in Book X he is a serpent whether he will or no. This progressive degradation, of which he himself is vividly aware, is carefully marked in the poem. He begins by fighting for 'liberty,' however misconceived; but almost at once sinks to fighting for 'Honour, Dominion, glorie, and renoune' (VI, 422). Defeated in this, he sinks to that great design which makes the main subject of the poem—the design of ruining two creatures who had never done him any harm, no longer in the serious hope of victory, but only to annoy the Enemy whom he cannot directly attack. (The coward in Beaumont and Fletcher's play, not daring to fight a duel, decided to go home and beat his servants.) This brings him as a spy into the universe, and soon not even a political spy, but a mere peeping Tom leering and writhing in prurience as he overlooks the privacy of two lovers, and there described, almost for the first time in the poem, not as the fallen Archangel or Hell's dread Emperor, but simply as 'the Devil' (IV, 502)—the salacious grotesque, half bogey and half buffoon, of popular tradition. From hero to general, from general to politician, from politician to secret service agent, and thence to a thing that peers in at bedroom or bathroom windows, and thence to a toad, and finally to a snake—such is the progress of Satan. This progress, misunderstood, has given rise to the belief that Milton began by making Satan more glorious than he intended and then, too late, attempted to rectify the error. But such an unerring picture of the 'sense of injured merit' in its actual operations upon character cannot have come about by blundering and accident. We need not doubt that it was the poet's intention to be fair to evil, to give it a run for its money—to show it *first* at the height, with all its rants and melodrama and 'Godlike imitated state' about it, and *then* to trace what actually becomes of such self-intoxication when it encounters reality. Fortunately we happen to know that the terrible soliloquy in Book IV (32-113) was conceived and in part composed before the first two books. It was from this conception that Milton started and when he put the most specious aspects of Satan at the very beginning of his poem he was relying on two predispositions in the minds of his readers, which in that age, would have guarded them from our later misunderstanding. Men still believed that there really was such a person as Satan, and that he was a liar. The poet did not foresee that his work would one day meet the disarming simplicity of critics who take for gospel things said by the father of falsehood in public speeches to his troops.

It remains, of course, true that Satan is the best drawn of Milton's characters. The reason is not hard to find. Of the major characters whom Milton attempted he is incomparably the easiest to draw. Set a hundred poets to tell the same story and in ninety of the resulting poems Satan will be the best character. In all but a few writers the 'good' characters are the least successful, and every one who has ever tried to make even the humblest story ought to know why. To make a character worse than oneself it is only necessary to release imaginatively from control some of the bad passions which, in real life, are always straining at the leash; the Satan, the Iago, the Becky Sharp, within each of us, is always there and only too ready, the moment the leash is slipped, to come out and have in our books that holiday we try to deny them in our lives. But if you try to draw a character better than yourself, all you can do is to take the best moments you have had and to imagine them prolonged and more consistently embodied in action. But the real high virtues which we do not possess at all, we cannot depict except in a purely external fashion. We do not really know what it feels like to be a man much better than ourselves. His whole inner landscape is one we have never seen, and when we guess it we blunder. It is in their 'good' characters that novelists make, unawares, the most shocking self-revelations. Heaven understands Hell and Hell does not understand Heaven, and all of us, in our measure, share the Satanic, or at least the Napoleonic, blindness. To project ourselves into a wicked character, we have only to stop doing something, and something that we are already tired of doing; to project ourselves into a good one we have to do what we cannot and become what we are not. Hence all that is said about Milton's 'sympathy' with Satan, his expression in Satan of his own pride, malice, folly, misery, and lust, is true in a sense, but not in a sense peculiar to Milton. The Satan in Milton enables him to draw the character well just as the Satan in us enables us to receive it. Not as Milton, but as man, he has trodden the burning marl, pursued vain war with heaven, and turned aside with leer malign. A fallen man *is* very like a fallen angel. That, indeed, is one of the things which prevents the Satanic predicament from becoming comic. It is too near us; and doubtless Milton expected all readers to perceive that in the long run either the Satanic predicament or else the delighted obedience of Messiah, of Abdiel, of Adam, and of Eve, must be their own. It is, therefore, right to say that Milton has put much of himself into Satan; but it is unwarrantable to conclude that he was pleased with that part of himself or expected us to be pleased. Because he was, like the rest of us, damnable, it does not follow that he was, like Satan, damned.

Yet even the 'good' characters in *Paradise Lost* are not so unsuccessful that a man who takes the poem seriously will doubt whether, in real life, Adam or Satan would be the better company. Observe their conversation. Adam talks about God, the Forbidden Tree, sleep, the difference between beast and man, his plans for the morrow, the stars, and the angels. He discusses dreams and clouds, the sun, the moon, and the planets, the winds, and the birds. He relates his own creation and celebrates the beauty and majesty of Eve. Now listen to Satan: in Book I at line 83 he starts to address Beelzebub; by line 94 he is stating his own position and telling Beelzebub about his 'fixt mind' and 'injured merit.' At line 241 he starts off again, this time to give his impressions of Hell: by line 252 he is stating his own position and assuring us (untruly) that he is 'still the same.' At line 622 he begins to harangue his followers; by line 635 he is drawing attention to the excellence of his public conduct. Book II opens with his speech from the throne; before we have had eight lines he is lecturing the assembly on his right to leadership. He meets Sin—and states his position. He sees the Sun; it makes him think of his own position. He spies on the human lovers; and states his position. In Book IX he journeys round the whole earth; it reminds him of his own position. The point need not be laboured. Adam, though locally confined to a small park on a small planet, has interests that embrace 'all the choir of heaven and all the furniture of earth.' Satan has been in the Heaven of Heavens and in the abyss of Hell, and surveyed all that lies between them, and in that whole immensity has found only one thing that interests Satan. It may be said that Adam's situation made it easier for him, than for Satan, to let his mind roam. But that is just the point. Satan's monomaniac concern with himself and his supposed rights and wrongs is a necessity of the Satanic predicament. Certainly, he has no choice. He has chosen to have no choice. He has wished to 'be himself,' and to be in himself and for himself, and his wish has been granted. The Hell he carries with him is, in one sense, a Hell of infinite boredom. Satan, like Miss Bates, is interesting to read about; but Milton makes plain the blank uninterestingness of *being* Satan.

To admire Satan, then, is to give one's vote not only for a world of misery, but also for a world of lies and propaganda, of wishful thinking, of incessant autobiography. Yet the choice is possible. Hardly a day passes without some slight movement towards it in each one of us. That is what makes *Paradise Lost* so serious a poem. The thing is possible, and the exposure of it is resented. Where *Paradise Lost* is not loved, it is deeply hated. As Keats said more rightly than he knew, 'there is death' in Milton. We have all skirted the Satanic island closely enough to have motives for wishing to evade the full impact of the poem. For, I repeat, the thing is possible; and after a certain point it is prized. Sir Willoughby may be unhappy, but he *wants* to go on being Sir Willoughby. Satan *wants* to go on being Satan. That is the real meaning of his choice 'Better to reign in Hell, than serve in Heav'n.' Some, to the very end, will think this a fine thing to say; others will think that it fails to be roaring farce only because it spells agony. On the level of literary criticism the matter cannot be argued further. Each to his taste.

14

SATAN'S FOLLOWERS

Hell is no vastness, it has naught to keep
But little rotting souls.

—EDITH SITWELL.

I had read Book II of *Paradise Lost* a great many times before I fully understood the infernal debate; and it is a pleasure to acknowledge how much my understanding has been helped by a remark of Miss Muriel Bentley's (unhappily not yet printed) which she gives me permission to quote. 'Mammon,' she wrote, 'proposes an *ordered* state of sin with such majesty of pride that we are almost led astray. Perhaps Milton has touched here so essentially the nature of sin that if it were not for the suspicious *live to ourselves* (II, 254) we should not recognize it as such, so natural is it to man.' This hint I wish to develop.

The difficulty of doing so is that I shall seem to be merely moralizing and even to be treating the poem as an allegory, which it is not. But the truth is that the aesthetic value of every speech in this debate partly depends on its moral significance, and that this moral significance cannot easily be exhibited without indicating those situations in human life which resemble the situation of the devils in Pandemonium. They resemble it not because Milton is writing an allegory, but because he is describing the very root from which these human situations grow. This needed no explanation when he wrote, for his contemporaries believed in Hell; but it does need explanation now. I therefore make bold to remind my readers of the mundane parallels to the predicament of the fiends. They have newly fallen out of Heaven into Hell. That is, each of them is like a man who has just sold his country or his friend and now knows himself to be a pariah, or like a man who has by some intolerable action of his own just quarrelled irrevocably with the woman he loves. For human beings there is often an escape from this Hell, but there is never more than one—the way of humiliation, repentance, and (where possible) restitution. For Milton's devils this way is closed. The poet very wisely never really allows the question 'What if they *did* repent?' to become actual. Mammon in II (249-51) and Satan in IV (94-104) both raise it only to decide that it is, for them, no real issue. They know they will not repent. That door out of Hell is firmly locked, by the devils themselves, on the inside; whether it is also locked on the outside need not, therefore, be considered. The whole debate is an attempt to find some door other than the only door that exists. From this point of view all the speeches begin to reveal their full poetry.

The kernel of Moloch's speech is in lines 54-58. Shall we sit 'lingering here' and 'accept this dark approbrious den of shame?' He cannot bring himself to regard the present misery as unavoidable. There *must* be a way out of these intolerable sensations; and the way out that occurs to him is rage. It is a way out which often occurs to human beings in a similar position. If the knowledge that we have betrayed what we valued most is unbearable, perhaps furious enmity against it will drown the knowledge. Anger, hatred, blind fury—these are pleasant compared with what we are feeling at the moment. But is fury safe? That does not matter. Nothing *can* be worse than the present. To rush blind-headed at the thing we have wronged, to die hitting it—this would be the best that could happen to us. And who knows? We may hurt it a bit before we die. Moloch is the simplest of the fiends; a mere rat in a trap.

Belial is less obvious. The key to his speech comes at line 163. 'Is this then worst?' Was it not far worse when we fled 'pursued and strook' by 'Heav'n's afflicting thunder?' Whatever we do, let us be careful. Some pains have begun to go to sleep, but a rash movement of ours might reawake them at any moment. We don't want that. Anything but that.

Our policy must be the very opposite of Moloch's—to be very, very quiet, to do nothing that might release the fierce energies of Hell, and to hope that we shall presently grow more or less used to it. Once more, this has its analogue in human experience. The actual moment at which we were wrenched out of our heaven, the fall itself, may be remembered as so appalling that our hell is a refuge in comparison. There was a moment when the traitor first saw the real nature of what he was doing, and that he was now committed to it; there was for the lover one last unforgettable conversation with the woman he had cheated. These moments were agony because in them he felt 'Heav'n ruining from Heav'n'—he was still a native of heaven himself, and the traces of honour and love were still in him. It is *that* state to which, at all costs, he does not want to return. The fires must not be reawakened: to grow numb, voluntarily to decline on to a lower plane of being, never again to admit any aspiration, any thought, any emotion which might 'dispell The *comfortable* glooms of Hell,' to avoid great literature and noble music and the society of uncorrupted men as an invalid avoids draughts—this is his cue. Of course, there is no question of happiness, but perhaps the time will pass somehow. Perhaps we shall reach Parolles' state: 'simply the thing I am shall make me live.'

Mammon goes one better. It is hard to select any lines as the kernel of his speech; it is all kernel. If I had to, I should choose the lines

> Nor want we skill or art from whence to raise
>
> Magnificence; and what can Heav'n show more? (272)

and what can Heav'n show more? In those words we read Mammon to the very bottom. He believes that Hell can be made into a *substitute* for Heaven. For everything that has been lost, you can find something else that will do quite as well. Heaven was magnificent: if Hell is made equally magnificent it must be just as good. There was light in Heaven: if we produce artificial light, it will be just as good. There was darkness in Heaven: why then should we dislike the darkness of Hell?—for of course there can be only one kind of darkness. This is why Mammon is called 'the least erected spirit that fell from Heav'n' (I, 679). He has never understood the difference between Hell and Heaven at all. The tragedy has been no tragedy for him: he can do very well without Heaven. The human analogues are here the most obvious and the most terrible of all—the men who seem to have passed from Heaven to Hell and can't see the difference. 'What do you mean by saying we have lost love? There is an excellent brothel round the corner. What do you mean by all this talk of dishonour? I am positively plastered with orders and decorations and everyone I meet touches his cap.' Everything can be imitated, and the imitation will do just as well as the real thing.

But all the speeches are alike futile. In human experience Mammon's plan or Belial's may sometimes work. But from Milton's point of view that is because the present world is temporary and protects us for a while from spiritual reality. But the fiends are not so protected. They are in the world of spiritual reality already and Hell is their 'dungeon' not their 'safe retreat' (II, 317). That is why none of these schemes is really going to work, why no device can possibly render their life endurable. Hence, like the sea sweeping away a sand castle, or an adult silencing children, comes in at last the voice of Beelzebub, recalling them to reality. And the reality to which he recalls them is this, that they cannot at all escape from Hell nor in any way injure their enemy, but that there is a chance of injuring someone else. Perhaps you cannot harm your country; but are there a few black men somewhere in the world owning her flag whom you could bomb or even flog? The woman may be safe from you. Has she perhaps a young brother whom you could cut out of a job—or even a dog you could poison? This is sense, this is practical politics, this is the realism of Hell.

Pope, praising Homer's invention, remarks that in the *Iliad* 'every battle rises above the last in greatness, horror, and confusion.' Milton deserves somewhat the same praise for his Debate in Hell. If we had only Moloch's speech we should have no conception of what was going to follow it. What else is there for impenitent and defeated evil to do but to rage and stamp? Few poets could have found an answer. But such is Milton's invention that each new speaker uncovers further recesses of misery and evil, new subterfuge and new folly, and gives us fuller understanding of the Satanic predicament.

15

The Mistake About Milton's Angels

> What philosophy suggests to us on this topic is probable: what scripture tells us is certain. Dr. Henry More has carried it as far as philosophy can. You may buy both his theological and philosophical works in two volumes folio.
>
> —*JOHNSON apud BOSWELL.*

Johnson finds a 'confusion of spirit and matter' pervading Milton's whole account of the war in Heaven. But Johnson approached it under a misconception; according to him Milton 'saw that immateriality supplied no images' and therefore 'invested' his angels with 'form and matter'—in other words Johnson believed that the corporeality of Milton's angels was a *poetic fiction.* He expected to see the poet's real belief peeping through the fiction and thought he saw what he expected. I once thought—perhaps most readers thought—the same. A new period in my appreciation of *Paradise Lost* began when I first found reason to believe that Milton's picture of the angels, though doubtless poetical in detail, is meant in principle as a literally true picture of what they probably were according to the up-to-date pneumatology of his century.

The great change of philosophical thought in that period which we call the Renaissance had been from Scholasticism to what contemporaries described as Platonic Theology. Modern students, in the light of later events, are inclined to neglect this Platonic Theology in favour of what they regard as the first beginnings of the scientific or experimental spirit; but at the time this so-called 'Platonism' appeared the more important of the two. Now one of the points in which it differed from Scholasticism was this: that it believed all created spirits to be corporeal.

Thomas Aquinas had believed that angels were purely immaterial; when they 'appear' to human senses they have temporarily assumed a body of air, sufficiently condensed for visibility (*Sum. Theol.* Ia, Q. LI, Art. 2). As Donne says, 'An Angel face and wings Of aire, not pure as it, yet pure, doth weare' (*Aire and Angels*). Hence, for Aquinas, an angel could not eat; when he appeared to do so it was 'not actual eating, but a symbol of spiritual eating' (*ibid.* Ia, Q. LII, Art. 3). And this is the view which Milton goes out of his way to controvert. When his Archangel dined with Adam he did not simply appear to eat, nor was his refection a mere symbol—'nor seemingly...nor in mist' (*i.e.* in a mystical or spiritual fashion. *P.L.* V, 435). Real hunger preceded, real assimilation, with a consequent rise of temperature, accompanied the meal. It is inconceivable that Milton should have so emphasized the reality of angelic nourishment (and even angelic excretion) if the bodies he attributed to his angels were merely a poetical device. The whole passage becomes intelligible, and much less poetically grotesque, when we realize that Milton put it there chiefly because he thought it *true*. In this he did not stand alone.

The root idea of the Platonic Theologians was that they were recovering from the ancient writers a great secret wisdom which was in substantial agreement with Christianity. Plato was only the last and most elegant of the six *summi theologi,* the others being Zoroaster, Hermes Trismegistus, Orpheus, Aglaophemus, and Pythagoras, and all these said the same thing (Ficino, *Theologia Platonica,* XVII, 1). That is why a Christian like Puttenham calls Trismegistus 'the holiest of Priests and Prophets' (*Arte of English Poesie,* I, viii). It follows that the miracles recorded of Pagan sages need not be either diabolical or legendary. 'The souls of men who have given themselves to God command the elements and perform the rest of those acts which poets sing, historians relate, and philosophers, specially the Platonists, deny not' (*Ficino, ibid.*,

XIII, iv). 'As for the miracles Pythagoras did,' writes Henry More (of Milton's own college), 'though I do not believe all that are recorded of him, yet those that I have recited I hold probable enough, they being not unbecoming the worth of the person' (*Defence of the Cabbala. Pref.*). Bound up with this is a belief that the pictures of non-human, yet rational, life presented in the Pagan writers contain a great deal of truth. The universe is full of such life—full of *genii, daemones, aerii homines.* And these are *animals,* animated bodies or incarnate minds.

According to Ficino each of the spheres and each of the four elements has, besides its general soul, many souls, or animals derived from it. They are corporeal enough to be seen, though we do not see all of them. We see the stellar ones because, though distant, they are bright, and the terrestrial because they are near and opaque. The aereal and fiery we do not see. The aquatic ('whom Orpheus calls Nereids') are 'sometimes seen by people with very sharp eyes in Persia or India' (*op. cit.* IV, i).

'I was always disposed,' writes Henry More, in his third letter to Descartes, 'to agree with the Platonists, the ancient Fathers, and almost all the magicians, in recognizing that all souls and genii, whether good or evil, are plainly corporeal, and accordingly have sense experience in the strict sense; *i.e.* by the mediation of a body.' How far he carried this idea may be seen from his book on the *Immortality of the Soul* (III, ix, 6) where he tells us that those spirits who have bodies of air may by 'local motion' and 'the activity of their thoughts' agitate the particles of such bodies till they 'scatter and perspire.' The body will then need 'a recruit'—'wherefore it is not improbable but that they may have their times of refection, for pleasure at least, if not necessity'. He even mentions 'innocent pastimes in which the musical and amorous propension' of such beings 'may be also recreated' (*op. cit.* III, ix, 4). It is true that in his preface (*para.* 8) he complains of this passage having been misunderstood; but he certainly did not rule out the possibility of an 'amorous propensity' in the most literal sense; 'that the genii or spirits which antiquity called gods might impregnate women' seemed to him 'not at all incredible' (*Grand Mystery* III, xviii, 2). Paracelsus thought the same of his Gnomes, Undines, Sylphs, and Salamanders, whose females are eager to marry men because they thus acquire immortal souls—and also for the more prosaic reason that the males of their own species are in a minority (*De Nymphis*, etc.). Wierus, coming yet closer to Milton, tells us in his *De Praestigiis Daemonum* that daemons have an aereal body which they can change at will into male or female, because of its soft and ductile substance. Burton, quoting Psellus, has much to say of aereal bodies, which 'are nourished and have excrements,' and 'feel pain if they be hurt.' If these bodies are cut 'with admirable celerity they come together again.' Bodinus, an eager upholder of the corporeality of spirits, holds, according to Burton, that the aereal bodies are spherical (*Anatomy of Mel.* I, ii, I, 2). Henry More agrees that this is their natural shape, but finding it difficult to imagine how 'two such heaps of living air' could converse, suggests that for purposes of social intercourse they temporarily cast their 'vehicles' into something like the human form (*Immortality*, III, 5). All authorities seem to agree in giving the airy body incredible swiftness and almost unlimited powers of transformation, contraction, and dilation. It is these bodies which explain the phenomenon of the aereal combat. I have never seen it, but in the sixteenth century nearly everyone seems to have done so. 'The appearance of armed men fighting and encountering one another in the sky,' according to Henry More, is 'most notorious' (*Antidote against Atheism*, III, xii, 7). Those are the 'airy knights' of *Paradise Lost*, II, 536, and the 'fierce fiery warriors' of *Julius Caesar*, II, ii, 19. Even a sceptic like Machiavelli mentions with respect the spiritist explanation of the phenomenon (*aerem plenum spiritibus et intelligentiis esse*) and affirms the phenomenon itself (*De Republica*, I, lvi).

With all this Milton was, of course, perfectly familiar. The Attendant Spirit in *Comus* is significantly called *Daemon* in the Trinity MS. The whole scheme appears to be assumed throughout *Paradise Lost*, except in one passage. In that one passage (V, 563-76). Raphael seems to assume the modern or scholastic view. After explaining that it is a hard thing to relate 'the invisible exploits of warring spirits,' he says that he will adapt his narrative to human sense 'by likening spiritual to corporal forms.' I am not at all sure that *corporal* here means more than '*grossly* corporal,' 'having bodies like ours.' The adaptation which Raphael promises may consist not in describing pure spirits as material, but in describing the material, though strictly unimaginable, bodies of angels as if they were fully human. But even if *corporal* be taken strictly, it will be noticed that Raphael half withdraws from his position before the end of the paragraph and hints that the spiritual world may be much more like the earthly than some people (for example, the scholastic philosophers) suppose. At most, this passage expresses a hesitation of Milton's, parallel to his hesitation between the two astronomies, a refusal to commit himself completely. Throughout the rest of the poem 'Platonic Theology' rules undisputed.

When once this has been grasped most of the inconsistencies which Johnson thought he had discovered simply vanish. When Satan animates the toad this does not prove that he is immaterial, but only that his subtle body can penetrate a grosser body and contract itself to very small dimensions. When he meets Gabriel he dilates. When there is insufficient room for the inferior angels in Pandemonium, they contract. There is nothing unreasonable in giving the angels armour; though their airy bodies cannot be killed (*i.e.* reduced to inorganic matter) because they re-unite after cleavage with such 'admirable celerity,' they can be damaged and hurt. A casing of some suitable inorganic material would therefore be a real protection. It is also reasonable (*P.L.* VI, 595 et seq.) that this armour, when opposed to the unfamiliar attack of artillery, should prove a hindrance rather than a help, by reducing the nimbleness of contraction, dilation, and locomotion which the aereal body would have had when unencumbered.

A certain amount of critical prudery, in which I once shared, has been aroused by the account of what More had called 'the amorous propension' of Milton's angels (*P.L.* VIII, 618-29). The trouble is, I think, that since these exalted creatures are all spoken of by masculine pronouns, we tend, half consciously, to think that Milton is attributing to them a life of homosexual promiscuity. That he was poetically imprudent in raising a matter which invites such misconception I do not deny; but the real meaning is certainly not filthy, and not certainly foolish. As angels do not die, they need not breed. They are not therefore sexed in the human sense at all. An angel is, of course, always He (not She) in human language, because whether the male is, or is not, the superior sex, the masculine is certainly the superior gender. But there exists among these creatures, according to Milton, something that might be called trans-sexuality. The impulse of mutual love is expressed by the total interpenetration of two aereal bodies; 'total they mix' because they are ductile and homogeneous—they mix like wine and water, or rather like two wines. The idea escapes the sensuality sometimes cast in Milton's teeth because the desire for total union, the impossible desire as it is for human lovers, is not the same thing as a desire for pleasure. Pleasure can be obtained; total interpenetration cannot, and, if it could, would be the satisfaction of love itself rather than of appetite. As Lucretius points out, men seek (and find) pleasure, insofar as they lust: they seek (and cannot achieve) total union insofar as they are lovers. I suspect that Milton had the whole passage in mind.

> etenim potiundi tempore in ipso
> Fluctuat incertis erroribus ardor amantum...
> Namque in eo spes est, unde est ardoris origo,
> Restingui quoque posse ab eodem corpore flammam.
> Quod fieri contra totum natura repugnat...
> Nequiquam; quoniam nil inde abradere possunt
> *Nee penetrare et abire in corpus corpore toto.*
>
> *De Rerum Natura,* IV, 1076-1111.

And obstacle find none, writes Milton of the angels; pointing by contrast the tragedy, perhaps the redeeming tragedy, of the human senses. No doubt these angelic fusions, since angels are corporeal, are not without pleasure: but we must not imagine it after the pattern of our own specialized and rebellious senses. Milton's angels are what may be called Panorganic—'all heart they live, all head, all eye, all ear, All intellect, all sense' (*P.L.* VI, 350). Whereas men have five distinct senses, each of which receives from the outer world its peculiar stimulus and converts it into its peculiar kind of sensation, these sensations being later united into a reflection of the world by Common Sense, angels, we are to suppose, have a single sensibility equally distributed through the whole aereal body and capable of picking up *all* those stimuli which are portioned out with us among the different senses, and doubtless some to which none of our senses respond. The mode of consciousness produced by such a single supersense is, of course, not imaginable to humans. We can only say that it would afford a much more complete and faithful reflection of the outer world than we enjoy.

I hope it will not be supposed that I am prepared to support Milton's angelology as science, if I suggest that it improves *poetically* when we realize that it is seriously intended—even scientifically intended. It should be approached as we approach similar scientific material in Dante. The *Commedia* combines two literary undertakings which have long since been separated. On the one hand it is a high, imaginative interpretation of spiritual life; on the other it is a realistic travel-book about wanderings in places which no one had reached, but which every one believed to have a literal and local existence. If Dante in one capacity is the companion of Homer, Virgil, and Wordsworth, in the other he is the father of Jules Verne and H.G. Wells. Moderns must not be shocked at this; the 'high-brow' and 'low-brow' branches of almost every art are usually specializations from an earlier and more fully human art which was neither or both. And something of this old unity still hangs about *Paradise Lost*. The angels are not to be judged as if they were the invented gods of Keats, but as poetizations of the glimpses which contemporary *scientific* imagination thought it had attained of a life going on just above the human level though normally inaccessible to direct observation. The details of Raphael's eating seem unfortunate to the modern reader because he judges them as if they were gratuitous inventions, to be taken on their merits as fiction. The whole point of view changes if we suppose ourselves coming to the work with a belief in such theories of the aereal body already formed and curious to see whether the poet will evade such details or triumphantly bring them in without becoming prosaic. When we find successful treatment of our own science in modern poetry I believe we are usually pleased: a future critic who thought that the theories of Freud and Einstein were simply poetic conventions—who supposed that the poet was producing them as the most beautiful and suggestive things he could invent—would probably form a different, and erroneous, judgement.

16

Adam and Eve

> Dr. Bull...wore a coat covered with heraldic animals in red and gold, and on his crest a man rampant.
>
> —G.K. CHESTERTON, *The Man Who was Thursday.*

'Adam,' wrote Professor Raleigh, 'from the depth of his inexperience is lavishly sententious.' When I first read these words they voiced a discontent with Milton's picture of our first parents which I had felt for many years. But I have lately come to see that I disliked it because I expected something which Milton never intended to give and which, if he had given it, would have gratified a somewhat commonplace taste in me and would have been hardly consistent with the story he had to tell. I had come to the poem associating innocence with childishness. I had also an evolutionary background which led me to think of early men, and therefore *a fortiori* of the first men, as savages. The beauty I expected in Adam and Eve was that of the primitive, the unsophisticated, the *naif.* I had hoped to be shown their inarticulate delight in a new world which they were spelling out letter by letter, to hear them prattle. Not to put too fine a point on it, I wanted an Adam and Eve whom I could patronize; and when Milton made it clear that I was not to be allowed to do anything of the sort, I was repelled.

These expectations of mine were due to my refusal to 'suspend my disbelief,' to take seriously, at least till I had finished the poem, the assumptions on which it is based. Raleigh's reference to Adam's 'inexperience' is misleading. The whole point about Adam and Eve is that, as they would never, but for sin, have been old, so they were never young, never immature or undeveloped. They were created full-grown and perfect. Mr. Binyon understands the right approach much better than Raleigh, when he makes his dying Adam say to his sons

These hands in Paradise have gathered flowers,
These limbs which ye have seen so wasted down
In feebleness, so utterly brought low,
They grew not into stature like your limbs;
I wailed not into this great world, a child,
Helpless and speechless, understanding naught,
But from God's rapture, perfect and full-grown
I suddenly awoke out of the dark.

(*Death of Adam*)

Adam was, from the first, a man in knowledge as well as in stature. He alone of all men 'has been in Eden, in the garden of God: he has walked up and down in the midst of the stones of fire.' He was endowed, says Athanasius, with 'a vision of God so far-reaching that he could contemplate the eternity of the Divine Essence and the cosmic operations of His Word.' He was 'a heavenly being,' according to St. Ambrose, who breathed the aether, and was accustomed to converse with God 'face to face.' 'His mental powers,' says St. Augustine, 'surpassed those of the most brilliant philosopher as much as the speed of a bird surpasses that of a tortoise.' If such a being had existed—and we must assume that he did before we can read the poem—then Professor Raleigh and, still more, myself, on being presented to him would have had a rude shock; it is *we* who would have been the stammering boys, shifting uneasily from one foot to the other, red in the face, and hoping that our clownishness would be excused by our ignorance. Dante strikes the right note:

And Beatrice said, 'Within yon light
The first of souls whom ever the First Cause
Did make, with love beholds the God who made him.'
Even as a leaf that in the passing wind
Bows its frail head and, when the wind is passed,
Of its own springy nature rises up,
So did I bow my head (stupendous awe
Was on me) while she spoke. But, strong desire

To speak to him making me bold again,
I soon began, 'O thou, the only fruit
That came forth ripe and perfect.'

(*Paradiso*, XXVI, 83)

Milton himself gives us a glimpse of our relations to Adam as they would have been if Adam had never fallen. He would still have been alive in Paradise, and to that 'capital seat' all generations 'from all the ends of the Earth' would have come periodically to do their homage (XI, 342). To you or to me, once in a lifetime perhaps, would have fallen the almost terrifying honour of coming at last, after long journeys and ritual preparations and slow ceremonial approaches, into the very presence of the great Father, Priest, and Emperor of the planet Tellus; a thing to be remembered all our lives. No useful criticism of the Miltonic Adam is possible until the last trace of the *naif*, simple, childlike Adam has been removed from our imaginations. The task of a Christian poet presenting the unfallen first of men is not that of recovering the freshness and simplicity of mere nature, but of drawing someone who, in his solitude and nakedness, shall *really be* what Solomon and Charlemagne and Haroun-al-Raschid and Louis XIV lamely and unsuccessfully strove to imitate on thrones of ivory between lanes of drawn swords and under jewelled baldachins. And from the very first sight we have of the human pair Milton begins doing so (IV, 288). Among the beasts we see two 'of far nobler shape,' naked but 'in naked Majestie,' 'Lords of all,' reflecting 'their glorious Maker' by their *Wisdome* and *Sanctitude*. And the wisdom and sanctitude, not in Adam only but in both, were 'severe'—in the sense in which Cicero speaks of a man as *severus et gravis*; that is, they were like a severe style in music or architecture, they were austere, magnanimous, and lofty, not remiss, nor free and easy, nor florid—a dry flavour, appealing to corrected palates. They are people with whom modern critics would be well advised not to take liberties. As Professor Raleigh (redeeming his momentary lapse) points out, Adam goes to meet the archangel not so much like a host as like an ambassador (V, 350 et seq.). That tone is preserved throughout their interview. If we think simply of a happy, naked savage sitting on the grass, then it is absurd that Adam should urge the angel to continue because the sun 'will delay to hear thee tell His generation' (VII, 101). This hyperbole is to be judged by the standards of exalted compliment from a great personage to an even greater personage on an occasion of high courtly festivity. Similarly when Adam modestly depreciates his own powers as a narrator and explains that all his talk is only a device to detain his godlike guest (VIII, 206), we are expected to admire the gracefulness of his courtesy—as the servants in Bercilak's castle expected to learn from Gawain the 'tacheles terms of noble talking.'

Adam's kingly manner is the outward expression of his supernatural kingship of earth and his wisdom. Of astronomy he is, indeed, ignorant, because Milton does not know whether the Ptolemaic or the Copernican system is going to be acceptable. But he understands the problems involved; his speculation has already roved over the whole created universe. When he received the homage of the beasts he instantaneously 'understood their Nature' and assigned their names (VIII, 352). He has complete insight into the mysteries of the soul and can give Eve a full explanation of the phenomena of dreams (V, 100 et seq.). His 'lectures' to his wife sometimes excite the smiles of the modern reader, but the joke is a shallow one. He is not merely her husband, he is the sum of all human knowledge and wisdom who answers her as Solomon answered the Queen of Sheba—'Adam, earth's hallowed mould, of God inspired.'

In considering his relations with Eve we must constantly remind ourselves of the greatness of both personages. Their life together is ceremonial—a minuet, where the modern reader looked for a romp. Until they are fallen and robbed of their original majesty, they hardly ever address each other simply by their names, but by stately periphrases; *Fair Consort, My Author and Disposer, Daughter of God and Man, accomplisht Eve, O Sole in whom my thoughts find all repose.* Is this ridiculous? At least it is much less ridiculous than similar formalities between *fallen* creatures in Milton's own time when husbands and wives could still address each other as *My Lord* and *My Lady* or *Sir* and *Madam* and the morning toilet of a French king was a ritual. Perhaps it is not ridiculous at all if we can once make the initial assumption that the reality whereof all such courtesies since the Fall have been simulacra, was present in Eden. This royal couple could live throughout in the grand manner. They uttered great verse *extempore* (V, 150).

This royalty is less apparent in Eve, partly because she is in fact Adam's inferior, in her double capacity of wife and subject, but partly, I believe, because her humility is often misunderstood. She thinks herself more fortunate than he, because she has *him* for her companion while he 'like consort to himself can nowhere find' (IV, 448) and obeys his commands 'unargued' (IV, 635). This is humility, and, in Milton's view, becoming humility. But do not forget that it is to Adam she speaks; a lover to a lover, a wife to a husband, the Queen of earth to the King. Many women in love, many wives, perhaps many queens, have at some time said or thought as much. Portia wished that for Bassanio's sake, she might be trebled 'twenty times herself.' A thousand times more fair, ten thousand times more rich,' and protests that, as things are, 'the full sum of her Is sum of nothing,' 'an unlesson'd girl.' It is prettily said and sincerely said. But I should feel sorry for the common man, such as myself, who was led by this speech into the egregious mistake of walking into Belmont and behaving as though Portia really *were* an unlessoned girl. A man's forehead reddens to think of it. She may speak thus to Bassanio: but *we* had better remember that we are dealing with a great lady. I am inclined to think that critics sometimes make the same mistake about Eve. We see her prostrate herself in spirit before Adam—as an Emperor might kneel to a Pope or as a Queen curtsies to a King. You must not think but that if you and I could enter Milton's Eden and meet her we should very quickly be taught what it is to speak to the 'universal Dame.' Even Satan, when he has said that she is 'not terrible,' is constrained to add 'though terrour be in Love And beautie, not approacht by stronger hate' (IX, 490). Even for Adam, though she is 'made so adorn for his delight,' she is also made 'so *awful* that with honour he may love' (VIII, 576; italics mine). There is no question, you see, of a boy and a girl tumbling on a bank; even for him there is that in Eve which compels deference, the possibility of *Daungier*. The angel hails her more ceremoniously than Adam. She stands before him unabashed—a great lady doing the honours of her own house, the matriarch of the world. Her grandeur, and a certain aloofness in her, live in some of Milton's most memorable phrases: 'with sweet, austere composure thus reply'd,' or 'to whom the virgin majestie of Eve.' Virgin, that is, in majesty: not, at the time to which the words refer, in body, and never virginal in the sense of being immature. Maidenly ignorance had never existed in Eve; in the first half hour of her existence she understood the purport of Adam's suit. She even understood it in all its bearings; you could not assume her consent, nor, on the other hand, would you need to ply her with Donne's metaphysics about soul and body in so natural an affair, though not one to be taken for granted: 'she what was Honour knew' (VIII, 508). She is able to share Adam's speculative interests. Such impress as art had made on the beauties of Paradise is largely hers, 'the hand of Eve' (IX, 438).

17
Unfallen Sexuality

> But doute, induryng that plesour
> Thay luffit uther paramour,
> No marvell bene thoucht swa suld be,
> Consyderyng thare gret bewte.
>
> —SIR DAVID LYNDSAY: *Ane Dialog.*

Milton and St. Augustine agree in contrasting the fallen sexuality which we now know, and which is conditioned by the disobedience of our members, with an unfallen sexuality. But for St. Augustine the unfallen sexuality is purely hypothetical: when he describes it he is describing what the act of generation *would have been* before the Fall, but he does not think it ever took place. Milton asserts that it did.

This difference is not very important, since there is, for St. Augustine, no reason why it should not have occurred. What is much more to the purpose is the saint's comment on his own discussion of the question. 'We are speaking of something which is *now* a matter of shame; and therefore, though we conjecture as best we can what it would have been like before it became shameful, it is very necessary that our discourse be rather reined in by modesty than assisted by eloquence. I speak of a thing which they two who alone could have experienced it never did experience: how then when mention is made of it *now* can it be presented to human fantasy except in the likeness of the turbid lust we have tried and not of the tranquil volition we conjecture?' (*De Civit.* XIV, 26) This was a warning to Milton that it is dangerous to attempt a poetical representation of something which is unimaginable, not in the sense of raising no images, but in the more disastrous sense of inevitably raising the wrong ones. This warning he defied. He has dared to represent Paradisal sexuality. I cannot make up my mind whether he was wise.

The difficulty is raised in its acutest form when Milton's Eve exhibits sexual modesty. Her impulse on first meeting Adam is to turn back (*P.L.* VIII, 507); she is led to the bridal bower 'blushing like the morn' (*ibid.* 511); she yields to her lover's embraces with 'sweet, reluctant, amorous delay' (IV, 311). Now Milton is here in a cleft stick. To readers since the Fall such scenes will hardly be pleasing if Eve is represented as having no modesty at all; on the other hand, shame of the body and the body's operations is consequent upon sin and had no place in the time of innocence. The defence of Milton's treatment must consist in distinguishing bodily shame as we now know it from some kind of bashfulness or modesty which can be conceived as existing before the Fall. Coleridge goes very far in this direction when he writes: 'There is a state of manners conceivable so pure that the language of Hamlet at Ophelia's feet might be a harmless rallying or playful teazing of a shame that would exist in Paradise' (*Lectures and Notes of 1818. Section VII: on Beaumont and Fletcher*).

It appears to me that we can, in fact, make some such distinction. People blush at praise—not only praise of their bodies, but praise of anything that is theirs. Most people exhibit some kind of modesty or bashfulness, at least at the beginning, in receiving any direct statement of another human being's affection for them, even if that affection is quite unrelated to sex or to the body at all. To be *valued* is an experience which involves a curious kind of self-consciousness. The subject is suddenly compelled to remember that it is also an object, and, apparently, an object intently regarded: hence, in a well-ordered mind, feelings of unworthiness and anxiety, mingled with delight, spring up. There seems to be a spiritual, as well as a physical, nakedness, fearful of being found ugly, embarrassed even at being found lovely, reluctant (even when not *amorously* reluctant) to be *found* at all. If this is what we mean by shame we may, perhaps, conclude that there was shame in Paradise. We may, I think, go further and suppose that even without the Fall sexual love would have excited this kind of shame in a specially strong degree; for in sexual love the subject is most completely forced to realize that it is an object. But that is quite the furthest we can go. All that part of shame which is specially connected with the body, which depends on an idea of indecency, must be completely ruled out. And I do not think it can be ruled out while we are reading Milton. His Eve exhibits modesty too exclusively in sexual contexts, and his Adam does not exhibit it at all. There is even a strong and (in the circumstances) a most offensive suggestion of female bodily shame as an incentive to male desire. I do not mean that Milton's love-passages are objectionable by normal human standards; but they are not consistent with what he himself believes about the world before the Fall.

Perhaps this was inevitable, but if so, the poet should not have touched the theme at all. I can conceive of a successful treatment. I believe that if Dante had chosen to paint such a thing, he might have succeeded—might have convinced us that our first parents were not living in virginity and yet prevented the false associations which Milton arouses. It is conceivable that Milton himself might have succeeded if he had said nothing about angelic love and treated the loves of Adam and Eve as remotely and mysteriously as those of angels. Even a protestation (and who could have written a better one ?) that he was now approaching the unimaginable, whatever actual treatment followed that protestation, would have gone far to save him. The trouble is that the poet hardly seems to be aware of the magnitude of his own undertaking. He seems to think that by twice using the word *mysterious* in this connexion (IV, 743, and VIII, 599) he excuses his very un-mysterious pictures—or to hope that when he writes 'half her breast Naked met his' we shall be able, without further assistance, to supply for Adam an experience both very like and totally unlike anything that a fallen man could possibly feel!

Newman complained that Milton treated our first parents with intolerable freedom. This is the opposite of the modern charge that he makes them inhuman. It is the better grounded of the two.

18

The Fall

> If you take a pack of cards as it comes from the maker and shuffle it for a few minutes, all trace of the original systematic order disappears. The order will never come back however long you shuffle. Shuffling is the only thing which Nature cannot undo.
>
> —SIR ARTHUR EDDINGTON: *Nature of the Physical World*, cap. 4.

Eve fell through Pride. The serpent tells her first that she is very beautiful, and then that all living things are gazing at her and adoring her (IX, 532-41). Next he begins to make her 'feel herself impair'd.' Her beauty lacks spectators. What is one man? She ought to be ador'd and served by angels: she would be queen of heaven if all had their rights (IX, 542-48). God is trying to keep the human race down: Godhead is their true destiny (703, 711), and Godhead is what she thinks of when she eats (790). The results of her fall begin at once. She thinks that earth is a long way from Heaven and God may not have seen her (811-16); the doom of Nonsense is already at work. Next she decides that she will not tell Adam about the fruit. She will exploit her secret to become his equal—or no, better still, his superior (817-25). The rebel is already aiming at tyranny. But presently she remembers that the fruit may, after all, be deadly. She decides that if she is to die, Adam must die with her; it is intolerable that he should be happy, and happy (who knows?) with another woman when she is gone. I am not sure that critics always notice the precise sin which Eve is now committing, yet there is no mystery about it. Its name in English is Murder. If the fruit is to produce deity Adam shall have none of it: she means to do a corner in divinity. But if it means death, then he must be made to eat it, in order that he may die—for that reason and no other, as her words make perfectly plain (826-30). And hardly has she made this resolve before she is congratulating herself upon it as a singular proof of the tenderness and magnanimity of her love (830-33).

If the precise movement of Eve's mind at this point is not always noticed, that is because Milton's truth to nature is here almost too great, and the reader is involved in the same illusion as Eve herself. The whole thing is so quick, each new element of folly, malice, and corruption enters so unobtrusively, so naturally, that it is hard to realize we have been watching the genesis of murder. We expect something more like Lady Macbeth's 'unsex me here.' But Lady Macbeth speaks thus after the intention of murder has already been fully formed in her mind. Milton is going closer to the actual moment of decision. Thus, and not otherwise, does the mind turn to embrace evil. No man, perhaps, ever at first described to himself the act he was about to do as Murder, or Adultery, or Fraud, or Treachery, or Perversion; and when he hears it so described by other men he is (in a way) sincerely shocked and surprised. Those others 'don't understand.' If they knew what it had really been like for him, they would not use those crude 'stock' names. With a wink or a titter, or in a cloud of muddy emotion, the thing has slipped into his will as something not very extraordinary, something of which, rightly understood and in all his highly peculiar circumstances, he may even feel proud. If you or I, reader, ever commit a great crime, be sure we shall feel very much more like Eve than like Iago.

She has still a further descent to make. Before leaving the Tree she does 'low Reverence' before it 'as to the power that dwelt within,' and thus completes the parallel between her fall and Satan's. She who thought it beneath her dignity to bow to Adam or to God, now worships a vegetable. She has at last become 'primitive' in the popular sense.

Adam fell by uxoriousness. We are not shown the formation of his decision as we are shown the formation of Eve's. Before he speaks to her, half-way through his inward monologue (896-916) we find the decision already made—'with thee Certain my resolution is to Die.' His sin is, of course, intended to be a less ignoble sin than hers. Its half-nobility is, perhaps, emphasized by the fact that he does not argue about it. He is at that moment when a man's only answer to all that would restrain him is: 'I don't care;' that moment when we resolve to treat some lower or partial value as an absolute—loyalty to a party or a family, faith to a lover, the customs of good fellowship, the honour of our profession, or the claims of science. If the reader finds it hard to look upon Adam's action as a sin at all, that is because he is not really granting Milton's premises. If conjugal love were the highest value in Adam's world, then of course his resolve would have been the correct one. But if there are things that have an even higher claim on a man, if the universe is imagined to be such that, when the pinch comes, a man ought to reject wife and mother and his own life also, then the case is altered, and then Adam can do no good to Eve (as, in fact, he does no good) by becoming her accomplice. What would have happened if instead of his 'compliance bad' Adam had scolded or even chastised Eve and then interceded with God on her behalf, we are not told. The reason we are not told is that Milton does not know. And I think he knows he does not know: he says cautiously that the situation '*seemd* remediless' (919). This ignorance is not without significance. We see the results of our actions, but we do not know what would have happened if we had abstained. For all Adam knew, God might have had other cards in His hand; but Adam never raised the question, and now nobody will ever know. Rejected goods are invisible. Perhaps God would have killed Eve and left Adam 'in those wilde Woods forlorn': perhaps, if the man had preferred honesty to party loyalty or established morals to adultery, a friend would have been ruined or two hearts broken. But then again, perhaps not. You can find out only by trying it. The only thing Adam knows is that he must hold the fort, and he does not hold it. The effects of the Fall on him are quite unlike its effects on the woman. She had rushed at once into false sentiment which made murder itself appear a proof of fine sensibility. Adam, after eating the fruit, goes in the opposite direction. He becomes a man of the world, a punster, an aspirant to fine raillery. He compliments Eve on her palate and says the real weakness of Paradise is that there were too few forbidden trees. The father of all the bright epigrammatic wasters and the mother of all the corrupting female novelists are now both before us. As critics have pointed out, Adam and Eve 'become human' at this point. Unfortunately what follows is one of Milton's failures. Of course, they must now lust after each other. And of course this lusting must be something quite different from the innocent desires which Milton attributes to their unfallen intercourse. Wholly new, and perversely delicious, a tang of evil in sex is now to enter their experience. What will reveal itself on waking as the misery of shame now comes to them (they are growing 'sapient,' 'exact of taste') as the delighted discovery that obscenity is possible. But could poetry suffice to draw such a distinction? Certainly not Milton's. His Homeric catalogue of flowers is wide of the mark. Yet something he does. Adam's hedonistic calculus—his cool statement that he has never (except perhaps once) been so ripe for 'play' as now—strikes the right note. He would not have said that before he fell. Perhaps he would not have said 'to enjoy thee.' Eve is becoming to him a *thing*. And she does not mind: all her dreams of godhead have come to that.

19

Conclusion

> Be war or ye be woo,
> Knoweth your friend fro your foo.
>
> —JOHN BALL'S *Letter.*

The purpose of these lectures has been mainly 'to hinder hindrances' to the appreciation of *Paradise Lost,* and appreciative criticism on my own account has been incidental. In this section I offer a very short estimate of the poem's value as a whole.

It suffers from a grave structural flaw. Milton, like Virgil, though telling a short story about the remote past, wishes our minds to be carried to the later results of that story. But he does this less skilfully than Virgil. Not content with following his master in the use of occasional prophecies, allusions, and reflections, he makes his two last books into a brief outline of sacred history from the Fall to the Last Day. Such an untransmuted lump of futurity, coming in a position so momentous for the structural effect of the whole work, is inartistic. And what makes it worse is that the actual writing in this passage is curiously bad. There are fine moments, and a great recovery at the very end. But again and again, as we read his account of Abraham or of the Exodus or of the Passion, we find ourselves saying, as Johnson said of the ballad, 'the story cannot possibly be told in a manner that shall make less impression on the mind.' In these dry and cumbrous periods it is tempting to see the nemesis either of that hieratic manner which I have defended or else of those heresies which I have pronounced uninfluential. But we should debauch our sense of evidence if we yielded to the temptation.

If those things sufficed to make writing dull the whole poem would have been dull, for they were there from the beginning. If we stick to what we know we must be content to say that Milton's talent temporarily failed him, just as Wordsworth's talent failed in later life. Mr. Yeats, in his Introduction to the *Oxford Book of Modern Verse,* says that 'but for a failure of talent' he would have been in the school 'of Turner and Dorothy Wellesley.' This is sense; he does not attempt to explain the failure. The truth is we know next to nothing about the causes governing the appearance and disappearance of a talent. Perhaps Milton was in ill health. Perhaps, being old, he yielded to a natural, though disastrous, impatience to get the work finished. And since he was writing in a very new manner, he probably had no useful criticism—no one to tell him that the style of these last books bore only a superficial resemblance to that of his epic prime.

In the second place, Milton's presentation of God the Father has always been felt to be unsatisfactory. Here again it is easy to look too deep for the causes. I very much doubt whether the failure is due to Milton's religious defects or whether it chiefly consists in giving us a cold, merciless, or tyrannical Deity. Many of those who say they dislike Milton's God only mean that they dislike God: infinite sovereignty *de jure,* combined with infinite power *de facto,* and love which, by its very nature, includes wrath also—it is not only in poetry that these things offend. To be sure, better men than Milton have written better than Milton of God; but the offence of his conception is not wholly due to its defects. And furthermore, I think the offence of his presentation is not wholly, or even mainly, due to his conception. The theological flaws (however we assess them) would not be *poetically* disastrous if only Milton had shown more poetical prudence. A God, theologically speaking, much worse than Milton's, would escape criticism if only He had been made sufficiently awful, mysterious, and vague. When the poet is content to suggest, our theological scruples are cast to the winds. When we read

> About him all the Sanctities of Heaven
> Stood thick as Starrs, and from his sight receiv'd
> Beatitude past utterance.
>
> (III, 60)

or

> Dark with excessive bright thy skirts appeer
> (III, 380)

we are silenced. It is when the Son bows over His sceptre or the Father entertains the angels with 'rubied Nectar' served 'in Pearl, in Diamond, and massie Gold' that we are displeased. Milton has failed to disentangle himself from the bad tradition (seen at its worst in Vida's *Christiad* and at its best in the *Gierusalemme Liberata*) of trying to make Heaven too like Olympus. It is these anthropomorphic details that make the Divine laughter sound merely spiteful and the Divine rebukes querulous; that they need not have sounded like this, Dante and the Hebrew prophets show.

In depicting the Messiah Milton is much more successful. Some objections here are based on confusion. People complain that his Messiah is unlike the Christ of the Gospels. But of course He ought to be. Milton is not writing about the incarnate Lord, but about the cosmic operations of the Son. The 'count'nance too severe to be beheld' (VI, 825) is, indeed, fully represented in the Gospels, too; but the scale and mode of operation are necessarily different. I must frankly confess, however, that I have only lately come to appreciate the War in Heaven at its true worth. The only preparation for it, in our days, is to read Mr. Williams's *Preface*. When I turned back from that remarkable piece of criticism to a re-reading of Books V and VI, it was like seeing, at last properly cleaned, a picture we thought we had known all our lives. From a proper understanding of Satan we come to recognize the true nature of the reply which Satan provokes from Heaven, and the very great success with which Milton has depicted its appalling majesty. It is, of course, important to realize that there is no war between Satan and Christ. There is a war between Satan and Michael; and it is not so much won as stopped, by Divine intervention. The criticism that the war in Heaven is uninteresting because we know beforehand how it will end, seems to miss the point. Insofar as it is a war we do not know how it will end; nay, Milton's God says that it will never end at all (VI, 693).

To many it seems that the, failure—even if it is only a partial failure—of Milton's God destroys *Paradise Lost* as a religious poem. And I think it is quite true that in some very important senses it is not a religious poem. If a Christian reader has found his devotion quickened by reading the medieval hymns or Dante or Herbert or Traherne, or even by Patmore or Cowper, and then turns to *Paradise Lost,* he will be disappointed. How cold, how heavy and external it will all seem! How many blankets seem to be interposed between us and our object! But I am not sure that *Paradise Lost* was intended to be a religious poem in the sense suggested, and I am sure it need not be. It is a poem depicting the objective pattern of things, the attempted destruction of that pattern by rebellious self love, and the triumphant absorption of that rebellion into a yet more complex pattern. The cosmic story—the ultimate *plot* in which all other stories are episodes—is set before us. We are invited, for the time being, to look at it from outside. And that is not, in itself, a religious exercise. When we remember that we also have our places in this plot, that we also, at any given moment, are moving either towards the Messianic or towards the Satanic position, then we are entering the world of religion. But when we do that, our epic holiday is over: we rightly shut up our Milton. In the religious life man faces God and God faces man. But in the epic it is feigned, for the moment, that we, as readers, can step aside and see the faces both of God and man in profile. We are not invited (as Alexander would have said) to *enjoy* the spiritual life, but to *contemplate* the whole pattern within which the spiritual life arises. Making use of a distinction of Johnson's we might say that the subject of the poem 'is not piety, but the motives to piety.' The comparison with Dante may be misleading. No doubt Dante is in most respects simply a better poet than Milton. But he is also doing a different kind of thing. He is telling the story of a spiritual pilgrimage—how one soul fared in its passage through the universe and how all may fear and hope to fare. Milton is giving us the story of the universe itself. Hence, quite apart from any superiority in Dante's art or Dante's spirituality (and I freely admit that he is often superior in both) the *Comedy* is a religious poem, a poetical expression of religious experience, as *Paradise Lost* is not. A failure in the last canto of the *Paradiso* would be disastrous because Dante is himself looking at God and inviting us to look with him. But Milton has only to describe how the angels and Adam looked at God: and a theologically inadequate symbol for God will not ruin the whole scheme—as in some large religious pictures it may be the position of the Christ that counts rather than the actual drawing of His face. No doubt the drawing of the face might be so bad that we could not get over it, and similarly Milton's God might be so bad as to spoil the whole pattern of which He is the centre. But I do not think He is as bad, or even nearly as bad, as that.

When these reservations have been made, the case of the *advocatus diaboli* against *Paradise Lost* is, I believe, complete. Its story, as treated by Milton, fulfils the conditions of great story better perhaps than any other, for, more than any other, it leaves things where it did not find them. The close of the *Iliad,* nay even perhaps of the *Aeneid,* is not really final; things of this sort will happen again. But *Paradise Lost* records a real, irreversible, unrepeatable process in the history of the universe; and even for those who do not believe this, it embodies (in what *for them* is mythical form) the great change in every individual soul from happy dependence to miserable self-assertion and thence either, as in Satan, to final isolation, or, as in Adam, to reconcilement and a different happiness. The truth and passion of the presentation are unassailable. They were never, in essence, assailed until rebellion and pride came, in the romantic age, to be admired for their own sake. On this side the adverse criticism of Milton is not so much a literary phenomenon as the shadow cast upon literature by revolutionary politics, antinomian ethics, and the worship of Man by Man. After Blake, Milton criticism is lost in misunderstanding, and the true line is hardly found again until Mr. Charles Williams's preface. I do not mean that much interesting and sensitive and erudite work was not done in the intervening period: but the critics and the poet were at cross purposes. They did not see what the poem was about. Hatred or ignorance of its central theme led critics to praise and to blame for fantastic reasons, or to vent upon supposed flaws in the poet's art or his theology the horror they really felt at the very shapes of discipline and harmony and humility and creaturely dependence.

As for the style of the poem, I have already noted this peculiar difficulty in meeting the adverse critics, that they blame it for the very qualities which Milton and his lovers regard as virtues. Milton institutes solemn games, funeral games, and triumphal games in which we mourn the fall and celebrate the redemption of our species; they complain that his poetry is 'like a solemn game.' He sets out to enchant us and they complain that the result sounds like an incantation. His Satan rises to make a speech before an audience of angels 'innumerable as the starrs of night' and they complain that he sounds as if he were 'making a speech.' It reminds us of Aristotle's question—if water itself sticks in a man's throat, what will you give him to wash it down with? If a man blames port wine for being strong and sweet, or a woman's arms for being white and smooth and round, or the sun for shining, or sleep because it puts thought away, how can we answer him? Dr. Leavis does not differ from me about the properties of Milton's epic verse. He describes them very accurately—and understands them better, in my opinion, than Mr. Pearsall Smith. It is not that he and I see different things when we look at *Paradise Lost.* He sees and hates the very same that I see and love. Hence the disagreement between us tends to escape from the realm of literary criticism. We differ not about the nature of Milton's poetry, but about the nature of man, or even the nature of joy itself. For this, in the long run, is the real question at issue; whether man should or should not continue to be 'a noble animal, splendid in ashes and pompous in the grave.' I think he should. I wish to see 'ceremonies of bravery' continued even in the present 'infamy of his nature.' The opposite view is held by very different people. A few comments on the reasons for which it could be held will conclude my book.

The lowest and most contemptible class (in which I include no critic whom I have mentioned by name) may hate Milton through fear and envy. His art is eminently civil. I do not say 'civilized,' for vulgar power and vulgar luxury have debauched that word beyond redemption. It is civil in the sense that it presupposes in those who are to enjoy it some discipline in good letters and good 'manners.' It demands that our merely natural passions should have already been organized into such 'sentiments' as ordered and magnanimous commonwealths prefer. It is not rustic, *naif*, or unbuttoned. It will therefore be unintelligible to those who lack the right qualifications, and hateful to the baser spirits among them. It has been compared to the great wall of China, and the comparison is good: both are among the wonders of the world and both divide the tilled fields and cities of an ancient culture from the barbarians. We have only to add that the wall is necessarily hated by those who see it from the wrong side, and the parallel is complete. From this point of view the decline in Milton's fame marks a stage in the rebellion of 'civilization' against civility.

A much more respectable class of readers dislike it because they are in the grip of a particular kind of realism. Such people think that to organize elementary passions into sentiments is simply to tell lies about them. The mere stream of consciousness is for them the reality, and it is the special function of poetry to remove the elaborations of civility and get at 'life' in the raw. Hence (in part) the popularity of such a work as *Ulysses*. In my opinion this whole type of criticism is based on an error. The disorganized consciousness which it regards as specially real is in fact highly artificial. It is discovered by introspection—that is, by artificially suspending all the normal and outgoing activities of the mind and then attending to what is left. In that residuum it discovers no concentrated will, no logical thought, no morals, no stable sentiments, and (in a word) no mental hierarchy. Of course not; for we have deliberately stopped all these things in order to introspect. The poet who finds by introspection that the soul is mere chaos is like a policeman who, having himself stopped all the traffic in a certain street, should then solemnly write down in his note-book 'The stillness in this street is highly suspicious.' It can very easily be shown that the unselective chaos of images and momentary desires which introspection discovers is not the essential characteristic of consciousness. For consciousness is, from the outset, selective, and ceases when selection ceases. Not to prefer any one datum before another, not to attend to one part of our experience at the expense of the rest, is to be asleep: the process of waking, and after that of coming fully awake, consists in bringing selected elements into focus. When the voice of your friend or the page of your book sinks into democratic equality with the pattern of the wallpaper, the feel of your clothes, your memory of last night, and the noises from the road, you are falling asleep. The highly selective consciousness enjoyed by fully alert men, with all its builded sentiments and consecrated ideals, has as much claim to be called real as the drowsy chaos, and more. That this chaos may furnish hints for a psychologist's diagnosis, I do not deny. But to conclude thence that in it we reach the reality of the mind is like thinking that the readings of a clinical thermometer or the flayed arms in a medical textbook give us a specially 'real' view of the body. And even if it were granted (which I do not grant) that the unfocused or unelaborated consciousness were in itself specially real, it would still remain true that literature which claims to represent it is specially unreal. For the very nature of such unfocused consciousness is that it is not attended to. In-attention makes it what it is. The moment you put it into words you falsify it. It is like trying to see what a thing looks like when you are not looking at it. You cannot make a true picture of that no-man's-land between the visible and the invisible which exists on the edges of our field of vision, because just insofar as you make a picture you are bringing it into the centre. I do not say that it may not be fun to try. There may be a place for literature which tries to exhibit what we are doing when will and reason and attention and organized imagination are all off duty and sleep has not yet supervened. But I believe that if we regard such literature as specially realistic we are falling into illusion.

Finally there is the class to which Mr. Eliot himself probably belongs. Some are outside the Wall because they are barbarians who cannot get in; but others have gone out beyond it of their own will in order to fast and pray in the wilderness. 'Civilization'—by which I here mean barbarism made strong and luxurious by mechanical power—hates civility from below: sanctity rebukes it from above. The round table is pressed between the upper millstone (Galahad) and the nether (Mordred). If Mr. Eliot disdains the eagles and trumpets of epic poetry because the fashion of this world passes away, I honour him. But if he goes on to draw the conclusion that all poetry should have the penitential qualities of his own best work, I believe he is mistaken. As long as we live in merry middle earth it is necessary to have middle things. If the round table is abolished, for every one who rises to the level of Galahad, a hundred will drop plumb down to that of Mordred. Mr. Eliot may succeed in persuading the reading youth of England to have done with robes of purple and pavements of marble. But he will not therefore find them walking in sackcloth on floors of mud—he will only find them in smart, ugly suits walking on rubberoid. It has all been tried before. The-older Puritans took away the maypoles and the mince-pies: but they did not bring in the millennium, they only brought in the Restoration. Galahad must not make common cause with Mordred, for it is always Mordred who gains, and he who loses, by such alliance.

Appendix

NOTES ON CERTAIN PASSAGES

I. 467. 'Him followed *Rimmon.*' The inversion could occur in prose. Cf. Daniel *Apologie for Ryme,* 1603. 'Him followed *Bessarion, Trapezantius, Theodore Gaza* and others.'

II. 1006. 'To that side Heav'n.' This is not a mere 'poetical periphrasis' for 'lower side' or 'bottom.' These expressions are avoided because there is no up or down in Chaos. Cf. 893.

III. 1-7. This is an example of the process whereby features that enter poetry for different reasons remain in it as 'the adopted children of power.' The original reason for offering a number of alternative titles in addressing a God was doubtless practical: you wanted to be sure of getting in the name he liked. The custom, once established, becomes a means of showing the power addressed in various lights to the reader while retaining the solemnity which it inherits from its original use.

74. 'Firm land...or in air.' Milton is trying to make us realize that, though the spherical outer jacket of his universe was like land, those walking on it would have no sky to look up at. 'Firm land, surrounded or enveloped in something that looked rather like water and rather like air, you couldn't tell which, without any vault of heaven such as we see from the Earth.'

299. 'Giving to death.' Verity finds no object for *giving* and concludes that it has the intransitive sense of 'yielding.' But his quotation from *H. IV, Pt.* II, does not prove that *give* (as opposed to *give over*) can have this sense. Better evidence, perhaps, could be found in Devonshire *yeave* (from *giefan*) 'to thaw,' cited by Professor Wyld (*Historical Study of the Mother Tongue,* 278). But it is not needed, for *giving* in the

text has as object *what Hellish hate destroys*. What Hellish hate destroys is Human Nature. What Christ gives to death is His Human Nature (cf. 246 and Mr. Sewell's important comment on that line). What He dies to redeem is Human Nature.

IV. 36. 'And add thy name.' On the stage Satan would have had to do this in order to let the audience know whom he was addressing. Would Milton have inserted these words if the passage had been originally epic, not dramatic?

241. 'Not nice art.' Cf. Seneca's description of the world in the Golden Age: *prata sine arte formosa*. Ep. XC.

V. 257. 'No cloud...with cedars crowned.' On the assumption that the Angel from heaven-gate looks right down through the 'manhole' in the cosmic jacket (*v.* III, 526 et seq.) it is just conceivablc that he could see the Earth inside and Paradise on the Earth. But it would be difficult for him to see any 'other shining globes.' I think Milton has here forgotten all about the enclosed universe of Bk. III.

349. 'Shrub unfum'd.' I think Milton is contrasting the practice of sweetening a room by fumigation (cf. *Much Ado* I, iii, 53, 'I was smoking a musty room') with the simplicity of Eden where the aromatic shrub in its natural state (unfumed) was sweetness enough.

VI. 236. 'Ridges of grim Warr.' I do not think, with Verity, that Milton has Shakespeare (*Lucrece* 1438) in mind. The whole passage is full of Homeric echoes, and the *ridges reproduce* πολέμοιο γέφυραι (*Il.* IV, 371, etc.). What *they* were, I do not know.

268. 'Misery, uncreated till the crime.' Cf. Donne, *Litanie* 10, 'Two things, Sin and Death crept in, which were *never made*.'

VIII. 228. 'Equal love.' Probably in the sense of Latin *aequus*, propitious, benign (*Pauci quos aequus amavit Iuppiter*).

416-19. 'You are perfect *simpliciter*. Man is not perfect in that sense, but only in his own degree (*i.e.* he may be a perfect man, but man is not a perfect being). That is why he has a desire to enrich his imperfect being by social intercourse with other members of his species.'

512. 'Constellations,' *i.e.* of course, conjunctions: not 'constellations' in the modern sense.

IX. 157. 'Of these the vigilance I dread,' etc. These four lines sound very much as if they had been originally written for the stage. (I may owe this observation to Mr. Fletcher, of St. Edmund's Hall.)

442. 'Not mystic,' *i.e.* not allegorical. Milton is protesting against an exclusively allegorical interpretation of *Canticles*. He thinks there were two real human lovers in a real garden.

482. 'For I view far round.' Again smacks of the stage.

506. 'Hermione.' Almost certainly *either* Milton's slip of the tongue while dictating *or* the printer's error for *Harmonia*.

686. 'Life to knowledge.' Verity takes this to mean 'Life in addition to knowledge.' But surely it is the A.V. construction as in 'live unto righteousness' (I *Pet.* ii, 24).

X. 329. 'Aries.' The sun was in Aries because *the Creatour of alle kinde Vpon this signe ferst bigan The world whan that he made man* (Gower, *Conf. Am.* VII, 994).

Index